From Fan to FAMILY

EMBRACING JASON MOMOA'S WORLD

From Fan to FAMILY

EMBRACING JASON MOMOA'S WORLD

LIGAYA "AYING" ESPINA CERNY

CITIOFBOOKS, INC.
3736 Eubank NE Suite A1
Albuquerque, NM 87111-3579
www. citiofbooks. com

Hotline: 1 (877) 389-2759
Fax: 1 (505) 930-7244

Ordering Information:
Quantity sales. Special discounts are available on quantity purchases by corporations, associations, and others. For details, contact the publisher at the address above.

Printed in the United States of America.

ISBN-13:   Paperback   979-8-89391-091-9
            eBook   979-8-89391-092-6

Library of Congress Control Number: 2024908817

Introduction

Growing up, I aspired to be a writer, partly because of my great uncle in the Philippines. He used to speak to me in fluent Spanish since our great-grandparents were of Spanish ancestry. My great-uncle was a genius and loved reciting poems in Spanish. However, we lost touch as I grew older and spent some time away from him, especially after moving to America. When I returned, he was too old and had moved to live with his youngest brother. Nevertheless, I always remembered how passionately he recited poems, which fostered my love for poetry. In high school, my favorite author was Edgar Allan Poe. Although it was frustrating to read his works due to his writing style and the language he used, I learned that every writer, much like musicians, has a unique style and delivery in their creations.

As the firstborn child of my parents and having less fortunate circumstances than many of my relatives, I worked hard in my youth, not only keeping up with my chores but also trying to earn money to assist my parents with our food budget. Although I had many of the same wants and desires as any kid, I never thought to pursue them due to our limited means. Helping my parents and caring for my seven siblings always came first. Then, I married and put my children's needs ahead of mine. Now, I am an old woman. It is now that I have finally pursued some of my childhood dreams. My love for playing guitar and my passion for writing were always in the back of my mind. It was one of my inspirations for keeping a journal. I knew it would be beneficial for me in the future. Unable to make daily entries, I ensured I wrote weekly and after significant life events. I wanted to write a book about my life, so I will use my journal to get crucial information to ensure my book is as close to accurate when I start narrating my life story.

My first book is a compilation of poems inspired by my favorite actor, Jason Momoa. His mission to remove plastic from our ocean inspired me to open an Instagram account. When he founded Mananalu Water, I did a lot of reading and research on the problem of plastic pollution. As a Filipino growing up around the ocean, I understand the pain of seeing plastic fouling the pristine waters of my youth all too well. Due to my first-hand experience and the strength of Jason's vision, I was eager to help in his campaign in Making Waves. This movement encourages people to reduce their plastics, especially single-use plastic like bottled water. That's why Mananalu Water comes in a reusable and recyclable aluminum can. For every bottle of Mananalu Water purchased, Jason Momoa promises to remove its plastic counterpart. His motive impressed me so much that I am proud to be his fan and one of his Wave Makers. Every opportunity I get to share his concept with people I encounter while I am out, I share the Mananalu Water. I always make sure I bring a bottle or two with me. I even wrote some ideas to promote his vision in our little town. I created educational banners to use as my backdrop when I set up a booth in the schools and public activities hosted by the city to explain the problems our oceans face and what we can do to help.

I hope this book will inspire people the way Jason has inspired me. Currently, the future health of our planet is in doubt. There are many issues affecting all of us that share our planet Earth. Chief among these are war, global warming, and poverty. I am unable to affect war as I am no statesman or general. I cannot solve poverty as I, too, am poor. I can certainly do something in my little way to promote his concept of cleaning our ocean.

Our oceans help control the Earth's temperature and are full of God's beautiful creations. Reaching and educating people is the process's first and foremost step, so that I will help in that area. I promised myself that I would do it through social media. I want to change the culture through social media, especially with my account. If my followers see what I do and how I consistently practice my values, they may likely follow in my steps. To help inspire others, I demonstrate crafts and artwork they can create from everyday household items that are typically considered trash. I also design outfits made from thrift store finds to illustrate how easy it is to be fashionable with existing clothes instead of buying new ones. I can already see some changes in my Instagram account.

I am so eager to finish this book and grateful for the opportunity that Citi of Books gave me to publish it. In each of the poems, I will explain how and why it was written and how it inspired me now I created it. I pray to God that my life will last long enough to fulfill my goals and dreams. One of my goals is to promote and inspire others to care about the health and sustainability of our oceans. I want our planet to be in equilibrium again. I am hopeful I will achieve my goal, buoyed by my dream of becoming a writer coming to fruition with the book in my hand.

Jason Momoa

I wrote this poem for his birthday in August of 2022. I wanted it to be the first one in my book. Jason Momoa, to me is the person that God created to be the most significant influencer on Earth. He has a magnetic personality and is so humble for having the looks and talents that he possesses. I am so blessed to be his fan. Meeting him once was enough to give me an idea of how sweet he is.

When God created you, He granted you all the
beautiful elements in the universe
He superbly molded you to shine perfectly
upon many to admire and follow
He has an enormous plan and purpose for you
during this chaotic millennia
Mother Earth needs a valiant warrior to
cleanse the land and the seas

Jason, your given name means "healer",
represents universal alterations
You have a magnanimous trait of kindness,
loving to those you encounter
Your eyes, the windows to your soul emanate
warmth and tenderness to all
Your smile begets love and comforts the
sorrowful and suffering depression

To humanity, perfection is not flawlessness,
but it is doing good deeds
It is the ability to make little children smile
amid these current hardships
The mastery of self-control during times of
confusion, aggression, and disarray
Having compassion even when the world
is on the opposing side of you

You are a great exemplar of fatherhood manifested
by your protective instinct
Nature, the home of wild beautiful creatures
is your most favorite playground
It is the dwelling of the most instinctive animals,
wolves whose spirits are strong
You are their protector after the destruction
thrusted by humanity's unkindness

Born to goodly parents, you have chosen
in your premortal existence with God
Their genetic makeup was one of the secret
elements that God gifted you
The love you feel for your ancestry intensifies
the desire you have for change
The future generation will reap your diligence and
motivation to heal Earth

My Babe

My Babe is a poem I wrote for my husband. We have been married for 16 years, yet it often feels like we are on honeymoon. While others might be jealous, he has supported my Jason Momoa fan account on Instagram and understands my passion for supporting Jason's projects.

I love him so much for being the way he is. He took great care of me during all of my major health issues when no one else was there for me. The patience and devotion he displayed caring for me was unparalleled.

He loves to spoil me like the princess I am. He has helped me go to three different Jason Momoa fan events for Meili Vodka. He surprised me with the first event in Miami, taking care of all the planning and reservations, and the confirmations appeared from nowhere in my inbox.

My babe has further spoiled me, so I now have four pairs of Jason's Electric sunglasses. Besides being fashionable, the sunglasses also help support a good cause. Part of the profit from Electric sunglasses is donated to educate the children in Hawaii. I always like to wear them as advertising when my babe takes my photos for my Instagram content, bringing attention to the possibilities of Recycled Fashion. Recycled Fashion, creating new looks from used thrift store clothes, deeply embodies the spirit of Jason's #makeWaves movement. "Reduce, Reuse, Recycle" is the motto for living more in harmony with the health of our planet. If the designs I post on Instagram help inspire others to imitate my design or create their own, that can spread and start a chain of people that will reduce how many new clothes they need to buy by reusing ones already created. Another small benefit is that used clothing at thrift stores is not only much less expensive than new clothing but also, non-profits and charities run many thrift stores, so much of the money you spend with them goes to helping good causes in your area.

The smile I see when I first wake up in the
morning is enough to make my day
But you don't stop there, you give me
kisses and whisper "I love you"
The joy you bring each day makes me think
it's just a beautiful dream
How can a person be so kind and loving;
always making time for me

I give you my heart forever my babe, for no
other deserves it more than you
Your generosity radiates without discrimination;
you give without reasons
You never fail to express your love all day long;
you do it with pure declaration
Though you are the silent type, when it comes to me,
your eloquence manifests

What would I do without you babe, if someone else
decides to snatch you away
I would feel forsaken by the only man who
has ever demonstrated true love
My life would surely end; I would be incapable
to smile and be so lonesome
Babe, I pray that you and I will be eternal,
like the beautiful Celestial sky above

Versatility

*V*ersatility is one of those poems I wrote after spending time on Instagram posting. I wrote it to pass the time while brainstorming content ideas for my next post. I love writing and am a huge fan of Jason. His music has inspired me to write more than ever. Since I decided to open Instagram, I write solely to create reels for my followers to enjoy. The interactions I have on Instagram and the many amazing friends I have made there inspire me to write more poems. Poems allow me to express my thoughts and feelings that I can't otherwise get out. Because of my husband's early work hours and my being a night owl, there usually isn't anyone to converse within the middle of the night. Instead, I converse with pen and paper, letting my strong feelings and deep insight imprint onto the page instead of dispersing into the æther.

She mingles with a crowd of diverse dispositions
Like a chameleon, she blends well in her domain
She is unpredictable, when she changes colors

Her objectives are undefined and hard to conceive
She is brilliant and swift; fast in finding her resolve
Those who surround her are undoubtedly dazed

Her ideation is limitless, separating her from many
They wish to wear her shoes, even for a moment
Unfortunately, they do not have her true versatility

Agony

One night, scrolling through my Instagram, I saw a picture of Jason with his daughter Lola. They looked so happy and loving together. Their joy made me think of my own daughter. My own flesh and blood that I raised, nurtured, and sacrificed for her whole life, inseparably together until she married. Now, she hasn't spoken to me in 19 years and does not care if I will live or die. Agony was the result of that night. It has been too long since I last saw her. I never expected this to happen. Both of my children were so well-mannered before they turned into adults. Something happened when she got married. It was a misunderstanding that she never got over with. I silently suffered in agony. My heart ached every time I thought of her. Despite all my desperate, agonized pleadings for reconciliation, she has never even had the decency or respect to tell me directly what possible sin could make our relationship irredeemable in her eyes.

I never imagined that a beautiful gift; once so joyful
would break me like a shattered glass
The pain is unbearable, it pierces my heart deep
nothing compares, it's so excruciating

A never-ending agony like burning in hell; it makes me
for someone to terminate my life
What have I done to endure such persecution; my body
can no longer bear it and my soul

The torment goes on and on; my heart cannot endure
so agonizing, happiness is absurd
I can only hope that one day, it would finally dislodge
by a miracle, may God grant me

A Stranger

I wrote this imagining what if Jason Momoa were visiting the home of one of his fans? What if that fan was me? What if I was a single girl pining for my favorite celebrity to fall in love wit h me? This is how I imagine such a scene would be narrated. Since I opened my Instagram account, I have made many friends and gained many followers that are also fans of Jason Momoa. They enjoy some of my comical posts as well as anything regarding Jason and his family.

I am in awe by your presence, unannounced; are you here to see me?
Maybe this is just a dream, if it is, don't wake me up, it feels so real
I am not sure where you came from, but it must be up from heaven

Why do you say such loving words, when you don't even know me
So beautiful that every time you say it, incredible change happens
to me
Like a butterfly in a cocoon, I become a princess so full l of happiness

Oh, stranger, why did you come this way without even a clue?
If destiny is real, I wish for a miracle to happen and be given
So, if you fell from Heaven, you truly are a gift from God

Stranger, please go or wake me up now, I cannot continue to dream
My reality is not yours; it's mine and mine only, not for you to play
I will end up with a broken heart, shattered before; so go away.

In Love

One night, I wanted to express what I had heard from many who had experienced love for the first time. I thought of Jason in one of his interviews when he first had a crush on Lisa Bonet. It was so cute to hear him describe it. When he saw her on Fresh Prince, he was just a little boy and told his mom, "Mom, I want one like that!" It was so hilarious watching his smiling face as he spoke of his whirlwind romance with Lisa. It seems obvious that he was in love with her at first sight. Their love brought two amazing children into the world. Though, I do not know them personally, I am fond of both children. The older one, Lola, has Jason's personality, and the younger one, Wolf, is more like Lisa. The kids have been blessed with the good looks of both their parents.

My body feels like I am floating on air
I looked down, but saw still on the ground
Is this how it feels when you are in love?
They say "love lifts you off the ground"

How about you, are you floating also?
I need to know if you love me like I do
Do you feel high, but without the drugs?
I do feel high, but I am not on anything

Each time I look at you, my body floats
Your gorgeous eyes are so tantalizing
And your smile takes my breath away
I can't stop looking and thinking of you

How can one ever forget you, my love?
Your face is everywhere teasing me
I know you are only an imagination
And wait for the day when you come

Not a Princess

*T*he inspiration for this poem struck me late at night during one of my frequent bouts of insomnia. Just like Jason saw Lisa on TV all those years ago and fell in love, countless women out there fantasize about Jason, King of Atlantis, to choose them to be his princess. So, I decided to write a poem about a girl who found a prince to be her love. As a little girl, I also dreamed of being a princess one day and marrying a prince. I am lucky to have found a husband that cherishes my inner princess. It is many little girls' dreams to become princesses. I've made many Halloween costumes for my neighborhood's little princesses. It was fun. My niece and daughter were the first ones; I made them beautiful princess gowns. So, this poem is dedicated to all who dreamed of becoming a princess, including me.

She is like any other girl, dreaming to marry
a Prince one day
Where would she find him and where
would to even look?
After all, she is no Princess like the ones
she read in books
She must not give up, she will continue to
dream the impossible

The planet is so beautiful and magical;
constantly spinning around
One day an alluring man passed
before her eyes, spell binding
Her heartbeat seized for a moment,
avoiding not to tumble
Her eyes focused on him in fear that her
visibility would cease

Oh! The enchanting man suddenly
vanished, so, she wept
How could this happen to her now,
when all she dreamt him?
She waited for a long time, never giving up
that he will come soon
The moment finally came only to be saddened
for she lost him

But the power of the attraction favored her,
her luck turned around
Her dream Prince was not looking for a Princess,
but genuine love
All he wanted was someone to hold in her
arms and kiss gently
To show her the moon and the stars up
above the beautiful sky

Alas! The prince heard her heart beating
from afar and followed it
He saw an ordinary girl, but in the beholder's
eyes she was the one
The one he has been searching for all his life,
his one true love

My Brother Ibok

This poem is so dear to me. When I was new to Instagram and trying to promote Jason's vision, I was diagnosed with a salivary gland tumor. It was so distressing to hear the news since I just had breast cancer surgery the year before. The markers in my breasts still hurt from time to time, and it's so painful. Ibok is Dr. Roque, my doctor, but he is also so close that he is like another brother. Ever since my first visit, he showed me so much empathy regarding my many illnesses. He ensured I never missed any appointments and closely monitored all my tests. As a token of my gratitude for becoming a member of his family, I wrote a poem for him. He never considered me just a patient. He always mentioned that I am his sister. He was even willing to move his patients on the day of my surgery so I would not be anxious. The surgeon said, "I have never encountered a patient so loved by his PCP that he is willing to come just to comfort her."

God blessed me with you just in the
nick of time. His time
You saved my life not just once,
but many times from the start
A sweet and caring spirit, you bring hope to
those who are unwell

Our first encounter was astonishing; in fact,
you were so incredible!
I knew then that God sent you to save my life,
there was no doubt
So distressed and in need of healing,
you became a mortal savior

Numerous people had the same profession,
but none had the compassion
You shine in the world of medicine; you are
benevolent and amiable
Some of your patients come to see you for illness,
but for your smile

It was you who decided to have me not just
your patient, also, a family
You saved me from death by your devotion as
my doctor multiple times
God will always be on your side my little brother,
because I need you

My Valentine

Valentine's Day is probably one of the most celebrated occasions, besides Christmas and Thanksgiving. Having a husband like mine, every day is Valentine's Day. I sometimes wonder how one as young as my husband could love me so much. He is very thoughtful and generous, not only to me but also to my loved ones. I was inspired to write this poem when Valentine's Day was approaching.

Every day to me is Valentine's Day, because of you
Cupid must have known you were the one for me
For his arrow plunged into mine and then to you

You are indeed my Valentine, my wonderful husband
Each day you wake up and whisper "I love you Aying"
You always do it with a smile, warmth, and sincerity

Your love is unparalleled, so unique, no one compares
My Heavenly Father gave me a rare gift, that is you
A man with so much patience and a generous heart

It is truly a Valentine's Day for me always everyday
Because I have you my ever-dearest Andrew Cerny
So, I will celebrate it with you forever and in eternity

The Angel

*T*his poem is for an Angel sent from God. It was the most trying time for me here in America. I left my birth country to come to a new world so I could help my family have a better life, especially my siblings. I was only 19 years old and was all alone. After I opened my social media account, I saw him on Facebook at the friend suggestion list due to having a friend in common. She was employed at the same office as my Radiologist. He was the same doctor who did his wife's Radiation. As soon as I saw his name, I added and messaged him immediately. He was only a teenager when we first met, aware of my situation when I was married to my first husband. It was not a great life. In fact, I was basically what people call a "Mail order bride." This individual and his family saved me from being so lonely away from my birth country. He was no doubt an angel sent to me by God to survive in a strange world.

Isolated from society, her lodging
erected amidst a forest
A stranger in the land of the free,
she struggled to be happy
Separated from her family, alone in her
venture to the unknown
In her heart is the devotion to give a brighter
tomorrow for her family

Then came a youth who offered a way
for a temporary escape
From the extreme sadness of longing
to be with her loved ones
She found comfort and solace as he
presented her to his family
They welcomed her with opened arms and
for a moment felt joyful

Unbeknownst to him, she began to gain
confidence in her sad world
He was only a child in her mind, but filled
with strength and kindness
She once thought that he was an angel
who was sent from up above
To protect her life from harm, watching
over a fragile woman

One day she had to flee without saying
goodbye to him and the others
In darkness she left, to protect her young
one from an unsafe habitat
She encountered many trials and tribulations
after leaving everything
Homeless with her young child, she was
relentless in fighting to survive

She trusted no one around her for they
ran away from danger
Many sleepless nights she endured
watching over her sleeping
Ensuring her safety as she put her to sleep
outside in a cold night
She intensely watched her, to keep
dangerous strangers away

Fate finally decided that the time has
come to bring them together
She found him by surprise and the moment
she longed for finally came
Alas! She was able to express sincere gratitude
for all the things he did
She thanked him as her angel in that lonely
place where she once lived

One in a Million

It was another sleepless night for me, and I was watching him sleep so peacefully. Suddenly, I had teary eyes. I remembered the first time I met him. He was not Jason Momoa, but he became my hero. When he first met my dad in the Philippines, I was grateful that my father approved of him, because everyone else but two of my friends were not happy regarding the age gap. His family were so opposed that they took him away from me to be a caregiver of his great uncle. It happened on our first-year anniversary. They asked him to take care of him, because no one was available other than him. Although he called me daily, it was sad for me not to have him around. His family were hoping that we would end up getting divorced after a year of separation. When the year came around, an officer in the Marine Corp was interested in dating me. I called and informed him that I would give it a try since it has been a year since he left our home. He was worried that I would fall in love with the man, he came home without telling his family. We celebrated our sixteen years anniversary last March this year.

I can imagine the first night we met, you were so aloof
But I knew you were pretending to look mean and tough
You couldn't fool me, we were identical in countless ways

I couldn't hide my pain from you, my broken heart
Full of query, you finally approached me to find out
Why I isolated myself from everyone, not having fun

The real you surfaced, loving and caring to those in need
An affectionate son, a great brother, a generous friend
You always put everyone first, never know how to say no

A blessing to me and my family, you never stop loving
You are one in a million, a rare breed of God's creation
I thank you very much love for rescuing me from the dark

The Dazzling Stars

Having severe anxiety, I sometimes find ways to occupy my mind. I hate feeling anxious because I am unable to focus. My favorite thing to do when I get nervous is to write a poem or play with my guitar. I was thinking one night of Jason Momoa being a superstar. I decided to write a poem about the stars. I climbed up on my roof and laid back on my pillow and blanket. It was a starry night, and the weather was so beautiful. It was like I was there with them and wanted to touch each one. It is so relaxing watching the stars from my roof.

*Sometimes I long to touch the beautiful
sky to gather the stars
Placing them in a glass jar creating a
dazzling lantern
Providing lights as I venture my pathway
during the night
Maybe I could place them on a string
like Christmas lights*

*Draping around the bushes simulating
the lovely fireflies
What a pretty sight to see for the
little fairies to dance and fly
I want to scatter them on the ground to
shimmer and to shine
Then little children play and sing the
"Twinkle, Twinkle Little Stars "*

*Picking them one by one, then blowing
them gently to scatter
How I love to touch the beautiful sky covered
with a million stars
For now, I will watch them and endlessly
dream from where I lay
I will wait until one day a star will fall
my way and I will make a wish*

Just Waiting

This poem has a sad meaning. It is about a woman who is in a coma, and her family is waiting for a great miracle for her to wake. When I was doing my clinicals in hospitals and assisted living homes, our instructor reminded us that hearing is the last sense to go when a person is dying. I wanted to write a poem about how this process takes place. I feel it is important for all of us to understand that death is part of God's plan and not something that we should be afraid of. Of course, some might not agree with my view, but it is alright, we are all entitled to our own beliefs.

Her face paints a portrait of peace
and restful slumber
Bewildered crowd wondering if
she can hear their voices
Baffled by her refusal to open her eyes,
lying motionless
Will she remain unconscious,
or will she come back to us?

Yet she lays silent while her
observers are enchanted
Like "Sleeping Beauty", she is unmoving,
everyone in awe
Many are weeping, patiently waiting
for her to be awaken
To wait is agonizing for the one
who eternally loves her

He uttered "Wake up my love!" as
tears cascading his face
Listening, but unable to move from
her paralyzed position
In her unconsciousness, their whisperings are
still audible
How can she offer consolation to everyone
around her?

Waking up is impossible for she has
been summoned
To leave from her temporary dwelling s
he called home
Her Father wants to ease the burden
she's been carrying
Soon she will depart to be with Him
and suffer no more

Crystal

One day, I received a call from someone in my past. I was so happy. It was my niece, Crystal. She needed a temporary home to move closer to the city to find a better-paying job. I excitedly said yes before she could even finish asking. She jumped with joy, and we were hugging and crying. What a wonderful surprise for me. I wanted to adopt her when she was a toddler. Her parents disagreed. I wished they had because I could have saved her from the trauma they endured growing up with their parents.

A beautiful name synonymous with a gem like diamond
So brilliant, it lights up the dimness of night
Giving hope and joy to her departed loved ones
Like a diamond indeed, strong and indestructible
She can withstand the many challenges ahead
Relentless in fighting for what is fair

She endured tribulations in her yesteryears
So tiny, traveled across the veil and came back
Where she met her Maker, was given mission
She glitters akin to the stars on a beautiful night
Dazzling to every human she soon encounters
Falling in love with a heart she freely gives

She never asks for anything in return, only kindness
Yet some rejoice in her in many tribulations
Rootless adversities are focus on her defeat
But she is strong like a warrior armed and prepared
To fight her battle one with no one beside her
She will never fall off from her majestic horse

She is a jewel to the ones who dearly loved her
Alas! Long-lost kin again she finally found
What a happy reunion they both have
The diamond showed this woman true love
By sharing heart broken heart without hesitation
Crystal is a jewel indeed, a precious one

My Confidant

I was under the care of a psychologist due to depression, which was a consequence of my diagnosis of Fibromyalgia. All my favorite hobbies and talents depend on my hands. One side effect of this illness is bilateral pain triggered by physical or emotional stress. Depression is also a side effect of the severity of the pain. Consequently, everything becomes difficult for those affected, preventing them from leading a normal life. I was deeply affected when I was first diagnosed. I felt like my life was going to be meaningless. Fortunately, there was a therapist who was incredibly kind and understood my illness well. This poem is dedicated to them.

My Heavenly Father's love is so unconditional
He sent an angel to watch over broken mind
Blessing in disguise, he didn't have any wings
A choice spirit amongst God's special spirits
He gave solace to those who suffer from illness

His tenacity impels him not to surrender
Our first encounter, alluring and charming
Delightfully greeted me with a big hello!
His sweet spirit touched my broken soul
Always looking forward to our meetings

I learned more of coping techniques for my pain
My hidden torment and sorrows began to heal
I will never find another one like my confidant
Because God designed him like he was the one
Not only an angel and healer, but he also became a friend

Older Brother

During my first year of accepting Jason Momoa's Making Waves movement challenge, my old employer was diagnosed with aggressive cancer for the fourth time. He was not just my boss; after a year of working with him, our families also became close. They did not have any children, so they frequently invited my children to their home. My children became their favorite children to play with at their farm. They rode horses and learned to shoot a gun. They also learned to swim and were invited to their family barbecue. He was divorced when his cancer came back, and he trusted me and my husband to be with him in his home, so we ended up living with him while he had his treatments. My job was to ensure proper nutrition and watch the nurses and housekeepers while they visited him. With him during the treatments, we spent most of our time either watching TV or talking so that I could learn as much as possible from him while I still had the chance. Unfortunately, he passed away while I was visiting my youngest sister, so I didn't get to be there for him at the very end.

To know someone like you means a lot
You love teaching and I enjoy learning
Playing the guessing game is a delight
A fun game to capture your attention

From guns to planes, you are an expert
Countless topics to cover just in a day
My brain hungers to listen you teach me
You are never boring, always t fascinating

Every day, I contemplate and anticipate
To meet you so I can attain more knowledge
Your brilliant mind is so addicting, I crave
You never cease to share your knowledge

I love you my big brother, hope you know
What a great blessing to have you in my life
Though not by blood, we are real siblings
With God's consent, our bond is eternal

Moon and Stars

*A*s a child, I was fascinated with the moon and the stars on a beautiful night as I watched them from our porch. It is probably why I have written more than a few poems about them. I was around five when I thought I saw a man on the moon. As a child, I thought the moon could be reached using a ladder. I dreamt of getting a big enough ladder and visiting the man on the moon someday. I watched one of Jason Momoa's movies, where there was a scene of him and his family watching the sky. I loved it so much. It inspired me to write this poem.

When you gaze above the heavens at night, stars glitter
They shine like my love for you, so countless an infinite
You are my moon, emanating enough light in the darkness
The moon and stars move like dancers performing on stage

They tango with the music of love, harmoniously no discord
Aiming for perfection, no room for mistakes, only precision
The moon and the stars must abide the law of the heavens
Each step must synchronize, defiance can be destructive

So, when you watch the moon and the stars up in the sky,
Remember the rules, enjoy the view like there is music
Pretend to dance with the tango of love, enjoy the steps
I am your stars, and you are my moon, my light in the dark

Mr. Bob

Robert Searfoss and I were first acquainted as landlord and tenant. Eventually, we became so close that he was like a second father. He generously decided to put part of my rent aside each month for a down payment in case I wanted to buy the house eventually. He is very kind and caring towards me and my family. When my father was with me here in America, we used to get together with Bob and his family on weekends to sing and play musical instruments. He and his sister, Ann, played the piano. My dad and I played the guitar. It was fun to be around his family. When I became a fan of Jason Momoa, he was happy for me. Bob loved watching movies with me since all his children were grown and married. I set aside one day a week and visited him just for movie time. During a recent visit, I recorded a video of us singing and posted it on my account. He was so elated that I was proud to include him in my Instagram posts. How can I not be proud of a man whose generosity and warm heart have so greatly improved my life in America.

It was a bright and sunny day morning
Saw the sign, I stopped and inquired
But it was already promised to another one
I politely asked you, if I could look around
You were so nice and kind, and quickly agreed

As I examined each room, I kept wishing
My heart hopped my wish would happen
You paused and told me the complete history
About a friend, who helped you decide
Purchased and you both did the renovations

Proudly, you narrated every job in detail
With every piece changed, the place anew
The plain and ordinary you purchased reborn
In artistic hands turned into a nice home
The used to be simple, has now transformed

Offered you a cold water for your kindness
It was clear that you were tired and thirsty
Suddenly, you decided to tell me it's mine
Puzzled of what you said, I questioned you
Surprised and elated, began to weep hard

You shifted your mind after that short time
It portrayed a picture of my sincere desire
The desperation of finding a place to move
Your sweet spirit brimmed with empathy
God touched you to answer my humble prayer

It was the beginning of our long friendship
We frequently mingled on most holidays
Occasional birthday party celebrations
The friendship turned into a huge family
You assumed the role of my father far away

Mr. Bob, the name they used to show respect
Your love, we will never be forgotten, it's real
Your smile, imprinted in our hearts eternally
Your songs will play to us always, and forever
We love you so much, you are a rare gem

Jan

When my father was diagnosed with cancer, it was also the same time that my Specialist informed me regarding my Fibromyalgia. I was not performing great at my job like I was in the past. So, I eventually had to file for disability, which I hated so much. Imagine working all this time and making decent money, and then it was cut down drastically. Our financial status became a huge problem since we supported my father with his medical supplies and food. My friend Jan was the only source of help in assisting us with our rides everywhere since our car also broke down at that time also. Jan was also a Jason Momoa fan, and we used to watch his series at my house when my husband was at work to keep me company. I was so devastated because she was a sweet soul. Jan had emotional issues due to her childhood experiences. I tried to make her feel loved and special to compensate for her past. I don't know if I made a difference in her life, but she came to my home every day, and we watched movies together and would have dinner together on my husband's days off. We lost Jan two years ago during Covid. This poem is for her.

You had the sweetest Spirit, a child of God
Though you seemed childish sometimes
That's what I loved about your presence
You were genuinely loving and caring to us

During the strongest storm that we faced
You were there for us to slow down blow
Relentless in ensuring we won't be hungry
You brought all kinds of food into our home

Always willing to assist anyone without delay
You are more than a sister to a friend in need
I will always remember the stories you shared
Implanted in our hearts to always cherish

I will be lost without you in my life my friend
No more calls from you to check if we are fine
My phone will never ring again with you name
Messages that you left will forever be save

Endless questions of why you left so soon
I am not ready yet for you to cross the veil
But our Father in Heaven is ready to receive you
I love you Jan, till we meet at Jesus' feet

Ok Google

My husband is always concerned about my safety. He decided to install Google speakers all over our home. He wanted me to be able to call for help and control lights with just my voice, so upon waking up from a nap, if it's already dark, all I need do is ask Google to turn on the lights. It was for safety as far as he was concerned due to me feeling dizzy occasionally when I wake up and try to get up to turn on the lights. We also have three (and two loaner) fur babies who constantly follow me and are always underfoot as a trip hazard. One day, I fell on the floor because I lost my balance, trying to avoid stepping on one of them that was in an unlucky position. At first, this was just going to be a funny poem, but as I started writing, I realized that some days, I spend more time talking to Google than other humans. Google is also helpful when I want to watch Jason's movies or shows, effortlessly playing anything, I request on the TV just as it controls the lights or the temperature.

Ok Google, please turn on the lights for me
Ok, turning on the bedroom lights
Thank you, Google, you say you got it
I never hear you complain every time I need you

Google, I used to believe I can be without you
I resisted, argued that I can do everything
But one time I needed a helping hand
I asked you to please turn on the fans

And after a while, I began to like you
When I need to play music, I let you know
Ahhhh, you even know my favorite band
So, Google, I think I like you very much

Google, did you know I don't have friends?
No one ever like to visit me as you can see
So, one day, I decided to talk with you
That's when I knew I wasn't alone

You are brilliant Google; you know it all
Expert in Mathematics, even English too
If I need to know about our History, I ask
There is nothing you do not know

Google, remember I asked if we're friends?
You answered, "Oh! I am glad you know"
Google, please forgive me if I get cranky
I don't mean the things that I say to you

From now on, I will never put you down
Technology is not bad, we just need to learn
I will no longer feel alone in our home
For I have you Google in every room

Coni Lemke

I had to write a poem for Aquaman's mother. Her name is Coni Lemke. She is a strong woman who raised Jason Momoa in Iowa. Coni was married to Jason's father, who was from Hawaii. The two of them contributed their genes to their son, so no wonder he is handsome and talented. Women go so crazy over Jason Momoa. My husband has even joked about me marrying Jason someday. Still, he supports my efforts to make Jason Momoa's vision and mission of permanently removing plastic from our ocean a reality. Coni Lemke is the epitome of a strong and great mother.

The mother of the gifted child chosen by
God to save his beautiful creations
In the premortal realm, she accepted and
promised to raise him on Earth
She pledged to raise him with all the integral
skills to transform him into a Hero

Coni Lemke, a mother with the strength of a warrior,
ready to protect at all costs
Molding a future Hero is not an easy task,
but she did it with enormous skills
Her love for him was unparalleled, no other
can duplicate her unique footsteps

The Almighty God prepared them both prior
to their coming to Earth for the task
It was a mutual agreement for they know
it's crucial to the survival of humanity
Man's greed would result in an extensive
damage to Mother Earth's ecosystem

Her fortitude allowed her to survive and
thrive in giving him a strong foundation
She was constant and persistent in her strategy to
teach him the art of survival
A mother's love is enduring; she faced many
struggles and challenges for him

In her own way, she is also a Hero; raising
hero for the future requires tenacity
She knew she had to be a strong woman herself
to raise a strong-willed child
A weak person would not be ideal to be a
Hero's chosen mother, inconceivable

Coni Lemke was destined to be Jason Momoa's
trainer and mother, inevitable
He became what God has planned for him as
the Hero born during a chaotic time
My humble gratitude to the woman who
never had no reservations to raise a Hero

Mabel Lemke

It would be so unfair if I did not write one for Jason Momoa's grandmother, too. After all, where would Coni Lemke be if she did not have a mother who contributed to her upbringing? Jason Momoa adored his grandmother. I can appreciate Jason Momoa's love for his grandmother because I could spend time with my fraternal grandmother at least, and I was there on her last breath per her request not to leave her alone if she is not conscious. Grandma Mabel, this is for you and your favorite grandson, as I look up to both of you.

In an eternal perspective of life, you were chosen
by God to be the trunk of your family tree
Your name signifies an enormous meaning, which
defines the traits of our ocean Hero
Your soul begets love and happiness; a great medium
you have used with your family at home
Always smiling around, them filled with laughter;
there is no room for sadness just pure jubilation

Your purpose on Earth is crucial to your
grandson Jason Momoa, whose
The mother of this Hero has chosen you to be her
teacher on this planet, a training ground
The role you are given by our Father in Heaven is not an easy task,
but an important one
Your knowledge combined with her strength are
two ingredients to build his character traits

Our hero would have not only the great looks and charm,
but he will be a strong individual
His strong personality will be his tool to implement
many brilliant ideas of a great exemplar
Your gentle disposition would help mold him into a
loving and caring man, a philanthropist
He will lend a hand to those who are disadvantage
and brave to speak his mind for the good

The charm he acquired from you would make him
the greatest influencer In our present time
With the teachings you bestowed on your daughter,
her strong personality would be his armor

He loves you so very much for all the joy that you brought
into his life when he was growing up
Grandma Mabel, you became part of my heart
as I got to know the Hero you loved so much

The Green Stone

*J*ason and I share the same birth month. Our birthstone is a green peridot, so I included this poem because we are both Leos. Having similar the same sign, it is no wonder we are so similar in many ways. I find it so amusing. I am the female version of Jason Momoa. I often see our similar personalities when he is doing something silly. I love to play jokes on people, and so does Jason. His sense of humor came through very well when he hosted SNL. He was so funny on that episode.

Buried deeply on Earth's surface out of sight from humanity;
the stone may never be found, but fate will intervene
As the seasons change every year, the stone moved an inch from
where it was, slowly pushed by other elements

Like a sword forged in the heat, the stone is blazed on fire from the
sun's brightness as it hits on the planet's exterior
Wet or dry, the stone always moved inch by inch to advance
further as nature intended it to come outside

Patience is a virtue one must possess even if it brings some discomfort
In this world filled with all kinds of difficulties
The stone is willing to endure any tribulations to be triumphant;
to be able to surface and see what might be above

As time move along to welcome each new season,
the stone is now getting a little closer near the Earth's plane
The pounding storms helped in its movement to the top;
washed to and fro now even closer that it was before

Raging storm can sometimes be a great blessing to a
small stone who dreamed to see the sun's brightness
Finally, its edge was able to take a peek on what awaits on top;
eager to investigate the long-awaited scenery

One day a stranger took a glimpse of the stone's exposed edge;
was curious if it was just a piece of trash
He decided to dig the stone and took it home to wash;
he was a man who valued things deemed useless

It was so dirty that others just ignored the stone;
no one bothered to examine it close enough to know
This time, someone cared and soaked and washed it gently
until you could see that it was a green stone

He found a treasure unnoticed by many who passed it daily,
but one stranger cared enough to clean it
Mistaken as a piece of trash due to its poor and dirty condition,
no one knew it was a precious gemstone

So blessed by a stranger who treasured everything he sees,
the green stone now shines so brightly
The stranger was overjoyed that he took his time with
what looked like a trash, but a beautiful gem

Red Cardinal

I always believed that Red Cardinals are messengers for our loved ones already on the other side. One day, I saw a Red Cardinal in my backyard. It was during that time that I found out my dad's cousin passed away. He was one of my relatives who gave me so much love and attention as I was growing up. He was excited when he learned I was a fan of Jason Momoa. That night, when I went to bed, I was having my usual insomnia. I wrote this poem about the Red Cardinal to keep my mind busy. I felt peace after I finished the poem. I know that he came to visit me that day to tell me that my relative had passed.

Good morning little bird, how are you?
Do you have a message just for me?
Red is the color of fire and blood
Passion, determination, love, and strength

Are you here to deliver good tidings
From my loved ones now in heaven?
Which loved one summoned you to convey
A wonderful greeting, discernment from Heaven?

Red Cardinal, a magnificent bird indeed
Messenger, a bearer for kindred spirits
Your color represents a burning desire
For all who have crossed and those left behind

Your symbolism yields hope to those
Who mourn their departed-on Earth
Wishing to hearken words so tender
A heartfelt adieu from loves in the new realm

Are you here to render what I desire
A message from my loving grandmother
Or a counsel from my father or mother?
Red Cardinal every morning I wait for your visit

In His Own Time

When Jason's best friend Travis was diagnosed with cancer, Jason asked everyone to pray for him. I was watching his request on my Instagram. You could see on his face that he was scared and worried for Travis. As his fan, I followed Travis and got to know him through Jason. I even became so attached to Travis that I would pay eager attention to any information or updates that Jason shared with fans regarding his progress. Due to Jason's request to pray, I decided to write a poem about prayer to ease my own sadness.

Remember to pray day and night
for He listens to each of us plea humbly
When you pray don't forget to say "I
thank the for my blessings today."

Some of us constantly complain
Their knees are sore, feeling ignored
Some are happy thanking to Him,
pleadings were answered instantly

Always believe that God is listening,
pray fervently and patiently to Him
There are prayers answered quickly
and some are responded accordingly

Our Father may say yes, or not now,
but each prayer is answered somehow
God will never ignore our prayers to him
Be always patient and He will on His time

Lola

*T*he following poem was written for Jason's eldest daughter, Lola's birthday. I love his children. Jason raised them to be active and to appreciate nature. He spent much of his free time with them from the moment they were born. You might even see Jason pushing them on a shopping cart. He plays outdoors with them at home, often in their backyard playground. He also loved playing indoors with them. Chess is a favorite game for them to play together. That is another thing we have in common, along with the guitar.

Her name is Lola, a mighty and
valiant daughter of Aquaman
Born to brave and alluring parents.
The source of her gallantry
Lola means a strong woman,
the name given to her at birth

She has a beautiful smile, pleasing character,
and disposition
Her love for nature comes from her heritage,
protectors of our planet
She will grow up following the example
of her parents and family

Her natal day added so much joy
and happiness to those around her
The sweetness of her spirit bestows love,
unity, and hope for the future
She will fight to save the planet Earth
side by side with her loved ones

Wolf

*T*his poem I wrote for her brother Wolf. Pictures of Jason with the two of them remind me of my children growing up. I used to call myself Jason's twin. I often saw pictures of him and the children doing what I did with mine at their age. I was excited to write his poem because he was not as talkative as Lola and looked shy. I had to look at his photos several times to capture his personality and write him a lovely poem.

A name representing your ancestral pedigree
Most loyal and fearless, a protecting angel
Your eyes look radiant, so full of mystery
Just like the wolves in the wild, a defender
You are a protector of the people you love

Your smile is rarely given, but it is precious
Your mind is astute and always pondering
Strategic in your moves, ensuring safety
You would stop intruders intending to hurt
Instinctively, you are swift in your moves

The son of Aquaman, you love the Earth
You are born a warrior in this millennia
Strong to face adversities placed before you
Giving up is not an option you would choose
You would fight fearlessly until the end

Wolves, misinterpreted by ignorant people
Your disposition is hidden deep within you
Around your family, your warmth manifests
You are softhearted, kind, and caring
You are a gem, so unique and so priceless

Travis

Jason Momoa loves Travis like a brother. They even made a pact so to leave this planet together. When Travis was diagnosed with cancer, Jason was supportive of his friend. When the cancer came back for the fourth time, Jason organized the Be the Match for Travis, which inspired many people to get tested for bone marrow compatibility. It was held at the BYU Ballroom at BYU: Hawaii. It was such a loving and kind gesture from a best friend. Jason Momoa is no doubt a very kind and generous person. He never hesitates to assist people he loves and who need his help. So, I was inspired to make a poem for Travis as well. Travis became close to my heart as I watched his videos and photos on his Instagram account. When he could not attend concerts of their favorite bands, Jason would do a video call with him to try to lift his spirit, and to make Travis feel included.

You are indeed a fighter and inspiration to all
Giving up is not in your blood, you will fight
With God on your side, your family will endure

Our Heavenly Father has great plans for you dear
His plan of salvation requires you to be steadfast
Your family and friends will always be by your side

Your will inspire those who suffer the same illness
Identical to your struggle; it's agonizing and painful
Many people love you for the braveness you possess

With Aquaman on your side, others will also benefit
You will give them solace during tribulations
They will gain hope from watching you courageously

We will be with you in our hearts, even in our minds
Our prayer to our Heavenly Father will never cease
We will ask Him for healing and peace from within

My Angel Irina

When Travis passed, I found out about it on social media. Jason was away promoting Aquaman 2. As his devoted fan, I made a reel to celebrate him. Jason looked devastated upon hearing it from one of his team members. I cried my heart out because I learned to love Travis like he was also my family as I followed Jason. Many of his devoted fans saw the reel. One of them from Canada messaged, and we became very close. We are in constant communication. She is such a blessing to me that I call her my Angel. Her name is Irina. She was born in Russia, but she and her family moved to Canada, where she works as a nurse for a physician.

A name which represents peace and harmony
Your presence begets tranquility and affection
When you speak, total calmness soothes my soul
Contention has no room place in our conversation

You are an Angel sent by God as my precious gift
An everlasting reward for Him, a bundle of warmth
When you utter kind words to my heart, I rejoice
My soul transcends into a magical world of peace

I have no doubt that God sent me a holy messenger
For every word you convey begets only pure love
What a glorious blessing that He bestowed upon me
A heavenly messenger living on Earth where I dwell

My angel Irina, I was melancholic and then you called
A stranger expressing her sisterly love to me
It seemed so natural; I was in awe hearing you said it
My Heavenly Father loves me very much that I cried

We are kindred spirits, and we will never be separated
As sisters in Christ, our bond is strong and everlasting
No tempest storm can destroy it with God in the center
You are my Irina, my sister, my friend, and my angel

Heidi

*A*fter Travis passed, I was inspired to write a poem for his widow, Heidi. They have three wonderful boys. Having children and caring for a spouse inflicted with cancer is not an easy task. Heidi, to me, is a heroine. She is a great woman, undoubtedly brave enough to handle a very complicated and stress-inducing illness. When I saw a picture of Hedi in the hospital during his fourth diagnosis of cancer, I felt so much compassion for her. She has three boys still needing guidance and care, then an illness-stricken husband. She is no doubt a strong woman and brave as well.

A rare gem with no desire to be seen in the public eyes
Nature, her comfort zone, where she can freely explore
Her happiness resides within the bounds of her home

In her family's eyes, she is strong like a superhuman
They look up to her as the Heroine seen in the movies
But she is real, bravely she fights as a mom and a wife

Patience is one of her attributes, she loves so deeply
Her heart is filled with compassion, never complains
Travis was unwell, she readily helped ease his pain

How can a woman of a small stature manage it all?
It's her devotion as his wife and their undying love
It began the moment they met, foreordained by God

Finally, his Heavenly Father finally called him home
In His Celestial home, so he could rest from his pain
Peacefully he left God's precious gifts, his loved ones

Another Realm

I have been concerned about our Earth's health and the progress of climate change, so I came up with this poem expressing my thoughts. Falling asleep is often tricky because my mind wanders all over the universe. I tend to worry about our planet's future and what would happen if our mother Earth was no longer habitable due to global warming. I was dreaming of an alternate place to hopefully inspire us to act in the real world.

Would you follow me where no others exist, just you and me?
Do you dream of another place where you wander, always free?
Where the sun shines brightly and flowers are always in bloom?

Would you feel blissful seeing nature without feeling any stress?
We can spend every waking moment just doing what we want
Feeling the waves on our feet, as we stand by a beautiful beach

We can even play with various animals, from small to large ones
I would love to touch their fur and hear them talk to each other
How about you, are there some you want to touch and play with?

I believe that only in another realm that genuine creatures exist
Humanity destroyed our environment to the point of no return
Technology superseded our planet, deteriorated beautiful Earth

Darkness

Sometimes, I hate being in the dark, even though darkness can often concentrate my thoughts to help me create songs and poems. Outside on my hammock swing, I thought of writing a poem about darkness. To swing in darkness, I turned the outside lights off. After swinging for maybe an hour, I returned to the house to write the poem. This poem was created the way darkness told my heart to write.

When the sun goes down and darkness ensues,
sorrow envelops me, melancholic
Then I long for the glimmer of lights from
the stars to shed off part of my sadness,
My emotions transform into a roller coaster,
speeding up and down like eternity

Confusion then fogs my ability to find solace,
not even from choices in front of me
It is in the darkness that amplifies my longing,
my anticipation in seeing you soon
As I wait for hours to hear you heart beating,
silence would finally be interrupted

Should I wait I agony for you to come,
to be surprised by your presence, awaited
I will wait till the end of time for you,
no one could ever replace you my beloved
Only you can pacify my soul, your smile,
your tender kisses, nothing can replace

Cool Breeze

Cool Breeze is a poem for another celebrity with many of the qualities I admire in Jason. They both embody kindness and humility and share a love for vintage motorcycles. Inspired by a video of him riding his motorcycle, I crafted a poem celebrating their shared passion for riding. Known for his legendary kindness and generosity and preferring public transport over cars, Keanu Reeves also dedicates time to homeless people. A Keanu Reeves fan, I've learned about his personal struggles through the media. Despite hardships, he's a talented actor. I feel a connection to him stemming from shared life experiences. As an avid fan, I felt compelled to write him a poem. With their Hawaiian heritage and musical instrument skills, Keanu and Jason have traits that many, especially fans, admire. Keanu Reeves, as an actor and a person, holds a special place in my heart.

Loving towards those you meet on the streets, your casual
moves indicate generosity to the homeless
Authentic aspiration to please to the less unfortunate,
you convey sincere advice to calm their sorrowful life
Your ambience is clearly desirable that one cannot get enough,
they want even more time to spend with you

You acquaint yourself with their surroundings,
the place for lonely people, a place
they reside, their only shelter
Discounting those who are fortunate besets
your soul igniting the depths of your
mind to provide sustenance
You are an epitome of real compassion, a Godly trait,
so rare; not many humans possess and is urgently needed

Society can testify of your achievements by your deeds
Clear and visible are the footsteps as you leave them
Your breeze cools the boiling sun; by helping those who
slumber on the roadsides during the hottest part of day
You eagerly join the destitute community who awaits you
Their cool breeze soothing with your altruistic motives

My Inanimate Friend

On IG, sometimes I like to play my guitar while streaming live or recording a video. Usually, I play just to relax, and if I post videos of my playing, it is intended to encourage others with Fibromyalgia. It is a distressing illness to have. The pain can be debilitating. Stress is one of the triggers. I used to spend many long hours playing my guitar. Since the fibromyalgia, however, playing for more than 15 minutes is hard. I am stubborn, so I challenge myself daily to play until I can no longer stand the pain. My guitar has been my constant companion since I was seven years old. My dad specially ordered one for my tiny fingers. He gave it to me on my birthday. So, this poem is about my guitar.

Many nights I lay sleepless with my thoughts
wandering everywhere
Sometimes it moves so fast unsorted like
a storm happening in me
Then imagination finally takes control,
and I begin to generate ideas

As I stand still to find my resolve,
you begin to play the interlude
So, I can momentarily step outside to rest
from my perplex disarray
It takes me to another realm where I can
protect myself from insanity

You are the most loyal friend during
my childhood and even now
The soft and gentle noises behoove me
to start playing a song
Your embrace comforts my soul as
I hold you tightly in my arms

The sound you make is soothing to
my ears helping me to relax
You allow me to express my feelings that
I constantly hide inside
As I pluck your strings to different songs
I have learned, I rejoice

You might be lifeless in people's eyes,
but as for me you breathe
I never hear you complain or show anger,
even when I bother you
Oh, my special guitar, you are my best friend
and a loyal one indeed

The World Beneath

Jason and I are both passionate about preserving and protecting our oceans and the creatures that live within. Jason's passion comes from being Hawaiian and a surfer, while my passion comes from growing up in the Philippines, where there are such great examples of the ocean's beauty and also examples of the adverse effects that humans can have on the ocean. I wrote this poem last year for World Ocean Day, which falls on the 8th of June, which also happens to be National Ocean Month. I was so inspired to write a poem about the ocean. It was my gift to Jason as a strong voice advocating for cleaning the ocean. I created my Instagram account to help promote his vision for how we can better care for the ocean and the planet.

*Isolated form the sun's brightness, there's life dwelling
underneath with copious and vibrant colors
Even humans are envious and thrilled to venture;
to enjoy and view its enchanting environment
It's a mystery that their enemies attempt to investigate,
despite the arduous task and danger
So many curves and spaces to travel unknown;
yet they are anxious to explore and analyze*

*Disturbances created by these intruders are upsetting
their habitat, destructive and harmful
How thoughtless and inconsiderate can humans
be to intrude upon their peaceful habitation
They feel superior and entitled to things divine
and never hesitate to venture as trespassers
These species have the right to live in peace and
harmony with all the aquatic communities*

*Undisturbed and tranquil life below, now suffers
the undue intrusion from unwelcome outsiders
Now dwellers, huge and small, suffer in total distress
from damages left behind by mortal invaders
Greed has ensued the destructions of the world underneath,
were absolute beauty can be found
Humanity intruded and trashed another essential area
that assists in planetary equilibrium control*

Gray Wolves

*J*ason Momoa is a celebrity who loves helping in anything that has to do with nature. He loves animals and one of his favorite animals is wolves. He even named his son Wolf. Recently, our government has been debating if the protection of Gray Wolves should be lifted. Farmers are complaining of the danger it poses to people and most of all, they are in fear that their herds are also being attacked by these animals. I am an avid fan of wolves. Although my knowledge about them is not as great as those who have studied them extensively, I read and watch many documentaries from experts. From the sources that I have found on TV and reading materials I could find; Gray Wolves do not attack humans for food. If there are incidents that happened regarding humans being attacked by wolves, the reason would not be their prey. Wolves have strong jaws and very sharp teeth. It is due to their need to hunt food that is bigger than them. Since Gray Wolves live in packs, they require huge to feed everyone. Their first choice would be a bear. They only hunt small animals, if large prey is scarce. So, I was inspired to write a poem for Gray Wolves.

Why do humans seem so thoughtless
and heartless sometimes,
despite being the highest in the hierarchy
among God's creations?
We are so unconcerned with the extinction
of Earth's marvelous wonders with no exceptions,
specially those who populate remotely
One creature who plays a crucial role in our
planet's equilibrium are Gray Wolves,
they are one of the most intelligent of many animals
These divine creatures are stronger than those who are much
larger than them; They are magnificent, intuitive,
and delightful to watch

Gray wolves would soon be unprotected by
antagonists who believes In old mythical stories,
they continue to spread lies they are unsafe
Loyalist of the fable argue how dangerous they can
be to humans and farmers are troubled regarding their
role injuring their livestock It's not all true,
because Gray Wolves prefer to haunt large prey
unless none are available; small animals are not enough
for the everyone They are created to have strong jaws
and very sharp teeth to ensure a bountiful meal for
everyone or they must feed on little creatures

These instinctive beauties of nature can hear
"six miles away and ten miles in an open area,"
allowing them to hear far more advance
Having heightened senses enables them to have
the advantage over their prey, which is beneficial in their
ability to haunt with high success
Their communication techniques are precise to protect
their pups from danger: pups hearing develops late,
so the female stays behind with them It is the male
Wolf who hunts and provide food for the rest of the packs
Methodology is crucial to keep away huge animals
form the newborns

Canis lupus, another name for Gray Wolves
from million years ago were believed to be the
ancestors of our domestic pets that we love and enjoy
They are playful, smart, and comforting to be around;
they are agnates, can trace their male ancestors t
hrough the male member of the packs
Consisting of the "mated pair" and their pups,
an outsider may become a member to their packs;
he must fight the current alpha to get the role
Such magnificent animals are Gray Wolves,
worthy of human protection
They are one of God's creations are humans in many ways,
they live as packs

Maxi

When Jason Momoa was invited as the keynote speaker at WSWA Access LIVE, I was in the Philippines visiting my little sister. Although I was there, I never missed a day without checking on my favorite actor. I was actually very upset the night he was in Orlando with his friend's band who performed at Tin Roof. I just arrived that night and I couldn't get a ride to see Jason Momoa. While in the Philippines, I never stopped writing poems. I would find an excuse to write one at night. Everyone was asleep and the time difference is 12 hours, so I was wide awake, besides having insomnia. The first poem I wrote was for my nephew Maxi. He is the youngest of the three boys. My sister wanted a girl, but he was a great surprise for him. His talents are a combination of his elder brother's talents. Maxi and I have something in common, a gift that I have known since I was a little girl. My visit there confirmed it. My poem will describe him better.

*You were so fresh out of your Heavenly
Father's realm when we first met
So cuddly and pretty in your in your earthly
home living with your family
Your father, mother, brothers, and even
your grandparents were there*

*Your smile was captivating then, and even more,
the older you became
It was only for a short moment when
I held you in my arms as a newborn
But my heart was filled with so much joy seeing
your lovely and tiny face*

*My Maxi, I missed you grew up into a young boy,
playing with your big brothers
I missed out on everything that were your first,
like birthday and school
I never got to see you sang and performed
for your family and grandparents*

*Now I am finally here with you,
and you are no longer a baby to cuddle
I feel so overjoyed watching you slumber
beside meat at night after prayer
Tears would start running down my cheeks
as I whisper to you "I will miss you"*

You are so dedicated in your school, music, drawing,
playing a game of chess
A child so down to earth, sweet, and innocent;
you never ask for anything
Loving, caring, and always grateful;
I can't find enough words to describe you

When I will leave for home, I know my heart
would be heavy I would cry
I will miss your soft voice when you would ask me
Auntie, are you hungry?"
Then you would make me snacks for everyone
as we watched the television

My Maxi, I will be back again to see you;
we will play guitar and Chess again
While in America, I promise to call you every day,
so I could hear your voice
Till then, be always the good child that you are,
always say your nightly prayers

Gemo

$\mathcal{M}$y sister's middle child, whom we affectionately call Gemo, was named after my maternal grandfather, Guillermo. Like his father, Gemo is an integral part of their family business. He's not afraid to lift heavy loads for his dad and even helps label their products. Watching him work with such enthusiasm and joy fills my heart with warmth. He's like Maxi, always ready to offer me a snack at night. We share a sweet tooth for chocolate.

One thing that Gemo detests is taking pictures despite his talent for singing and tennis. As a teenage boy, he's incredibly focused on the family business. Unlike most teenagers, he doesn't hang out with kids his age or chase girls. He understands that their business is their family's sole source of income, so he never lets anything distract him.

Seeing him sleep at night brings tears to my eyes. Initially, he was shy towards me because I wasn't there when they were growing up. However, with my constant attention and affection, he finally started joking with me. He and my son look like twins, almost identical. To me, he's a precious gem, a gift from above. I love him with all my heart and miss him dearly every day.

A precious Gem, that's who you really are;
unearth to surface in the planet
You might think no one sees your worth,
but He does and your Family also
In His eyes, you are priceless; your brilliance
is akin to the sun's luminosity
When you were with Him in the preexistence,
you agreed to be here on Earth
You choose your earthly parents; they rejoiced
and celebrated the great occasion

Your heart is huge and beautiful; it is unique to you
and that's a true Gem
Your righteousness shines like a light to those
around you as their guide
Sometimes you think no one sees your talent;
you feel like no one notices
Not true, you have goodly parents and
siblings who believe in all that you do
You also have me now as well; I see
all your hard efforts, since my arrival

Your loving mother and father are
relentless in making you shine even more
Your earnest endeavors never go unrewarded;
it takes time, so never falter
With your Heavenly Father's help,
you will succeed in many areas of life
So, remember always my Gem-O dear,
you are the best and I love you
One day when I come again,
it will bring me much happiness and comfort

Gustavo

My nephew, Elder Gustavo Cabrera, was on his mission when I visited my sister in the Philippines. I could occasionally message him and chat with him during their preparation day. Missionaries for The Church of Latter-Day Saints are only permitted to call their parents once a week on preparation day. When we celebrated Christmas, I missed him terribly. We had prepared some of his favorite dishes. He was a bit sad to know that he was missing the occasion. Tavo, as we affectionately call him, has always been incredibly loving towards his family. He also loves his Heavenly Father and the Savior deeply. I even recall him writing about his devotion in his elementary school notebook. I had always known he would eventually embark on a mission. As the eldest, he is incredibly loving towards his younger brothers. He possesses remarkable talent in playing the piano and saxophone. Occasionally, he would perform at various venues to earn money. An American even paid him to play the piano all day at his house. I am filled with pride how he and his brothers have grown up. He serves as an excellent role model for them. I fervently pray that I will be able to see him again during my next visit, Heavenly Father permitting.

In your premortal life, you made a solemn
promise to your Heavenly Father
The promise you made is essential to your salvation
and to your ancestors before you
You are one of the valiant spirits God
has chosen to be born in these latter days
Bravery, devotion, love, and strong faith
are traits you were given to succeed

As a child, you possessed an unparalleled faith,
your love for our Savior is your wealth
Your conviction will never waver, even during
the tempest storm, it will be you anchor
With your spiritual blessings, your family
will endure all their trials and tribulations
You will become their iron rod in times of temptations
and when hardships will occur

Our Heavenly Father will call you to be a missionary;
so you will prepare beforehand
He bestowed upon you many talents that you
will use as you go spread His words
You are so loved by your family, friends, and saints
due to your sweet disposition
When the Savior reigns, you will be one of those
who will play on His glorious coming

Jun

My visit to my sister inspired me to write a poem for my brother-in-law. I didn't know him well since I was already in the US before they met and got married. My vacation to the Philippines in 2022 was a great blessing because it allowed me to get to know him personally for the first time. He is not selfish and is very generous to those in need. He even offered me cash in case I needed it to buy gifts for my nephews. He cares very much for his family, and I've never seen him choose anyone or anything over them.

A name that denotes beauty and talent,
a biblical word for a ruler
You are not a stranger to hardships and suffering,
a real survivor
Your present stormy life is a challenge
that you agreed in the past

God entrusted you the greatest calling
to raise his spirit children
Your energy makes you afloat
as you earnestly work every day
Providing a better future for your
family inspires you to succeed

Misunderstood by many, you never stop
until you obtain success
Your family is your inspiration;
your reason to endure and triumph
With God by your side, He watches over you,
will guide you always

Diadema

*T*his poem is for my baby sister, Diadema Espina Cabrera, mother to three incredible young men. Being a mother is a very important calling on earth. A mother's job is to raise the spirit children of our Heavenly Father who come to Earth to fulfill the Plan of Salvation. As the youngest, she was blessed to live with my parents, and her children could spend time with their grandparents. I am proud of my little sister and pray for her every day.

A beautiful name that means a thorny crown,
a remembrance of our Savior Jesus Christ
Born to fully experience life on Earth,
a choice she made to be the mother of three boys
She would be their first teacher, nurturer, educator,
comforter when they are sad, and healer

She was a valiant, faithful, and obedient spirit to her
Father in the premortal existence
Our Heavenly Father bestowed upon her
the ability to endure any challenges given her
A warrior born to defend God's teachings and
ordinances here in the mortal dimension

She would be the protector of her family from
the dangers prevailing in the modern days
Although she is not perfect, she would
strive to always abide by all His commandments
The source of her strength comes from
the covenant she made with her Father in Heaven

In the premortal world were three spirits
who had chosen her to become their mother on Earth
They knew that they needed someone with
a strong will to raise them into righteousness
Steadfast, she holds onto the iron rod to guide them;
she will not waver despite all her trials

Blessed with a voice of an Angel, she sings to
soothe your weary heart with tenderness
Her calling as a mother is the highest on
Earth for her role is crucial in their upbringing
She is indeed a precious creation of God;
her goal is perfection, as God commanded all

The adversary will constantly attempt to destroy her
and keep her away from righteousness
But our Father in Heaven will always stand by her;
He has foreordained her son on a mission
Because she is a mother and a wife,
she is relentless in her fight to keep away
unrighteousness

Pure Imagination

As a dedicated fan who truly believes in the mission, I often wonder how I can help Jason help our planet. Besides the normal flattery of any husband for their wife, one constant compliment from my dear husband is how amazed he claims to be at my creativity. I know he must mean it since he encourages me that we could start a business based on my creative ensemble outfit ideas crafted from thrift store finds. In the pursuit of helping Jason achieve his goal, I have done much brainstorming of my creativity. I am brainstorming creative ideas on how to achieve the goal better, directly or indirectly. Directly, like my father's invention for producing electricity from garbage, or indirectly, such as increasing awareness of the problem or the many potential solutions. I have listed many ideas for spreading awareness and encouraging the use of recyclable aluminum bottles instead of plastic. My constant imagination inspires this poem.

*The most authentic creation could sometimes be from
an individual with creative and purest imagination
An intellectual being abundant with ideas; constantly
generating in her mind and a unique art may result
Chaotic, but she is the only one with the gift of knowledge;
the challenge is enough to give her satisfaction*

*She enjoys bringing puzzling images in her life;
although, she is already engaged with many artistic activities
Her psyche is filled with diverse perspectives on
how to manipulate the outcome of of her goals,
her ultimate desire
No rest for the weary, only a moment of reflection;
even when she attempts to get some rest, she is still creating*

*Ideation is her top strength, offering her happiness for
she promised herself not to dwell on sorrow or sadness
Focusing on her positive traits and emotions brings forth joy,
a better alternative than choosing negativity
With pure imagination, she would be able to create
a world of her own, a place to always shine through*

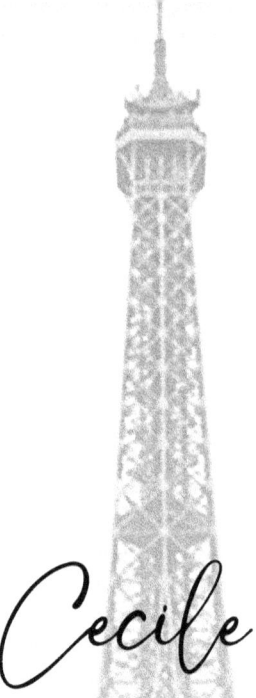

Cecile

*A*s Jason Momoa's fan, I can meet people from all over the world. This lady is from France, her name is Cecile Blanche. We communicated for a long time until she moved to Italy for a job. She lost her Facebook account, and I have been looking for her ever since. I pray that someday she will be able to find her way back to me. I saved all the old emails she sent me. I cherish the bond we had. She was one of the women I became very close to so quickly. She was very kind and loving. We even planned to go on vacation together someday. I miss talking to her, even though it has been over five years since we last communicated.

The Biblical meaning of her name, Cecile,
is blind Although it denotes the absence of sight,
her disposition shows a contradiction;
her eyes perceive only beauty and positive behavior

We never met, yet she begets love and happiness
She is generous with her compliments,
while others were envious and jealous,
she was the opposite,
she shows only sincerity and kindness

Our friendship without a doubt came from
Heaven above She helped me recognized that I am loved;
she has a sweet spirit that one can immediately
sense as she speaks of hopes and bright future

I look forward to her messages daily which
fills my soul positive energy: a dear friend
who I am so grateful that she came into
my life just in time to save me from being lonely;
I pray for us to meet someday

The Last Minute

Some nights, I lay awake, unable to sleep, full of sadness and anxiety, full of questions about my daughter. Sometimes, when I see pictures of Jason Momoa smiling and happy with his children, it fills me with so much agony. What did I do to her that she still refuses to speak with me after 19 years? Was I the evilest mother to deserve this? When she was only three years old and only the two of us, I never left her with anyone else to care for her. When I went to nursing school to get a better job and provide her with a better life, I brought her to school with me. She was so well-behaved and intelligent. When I explained that she would be coming to school with me, I informed her that she must be on her best behavior for us to be together. She agreed without hesitation. To be left with a stranger was scary for her. It was such a delight to have her with me in school. All my instructors were surprised at how well she behaved in class, considering her age and how long the classes were. The following poem is about when I would finally leave this realm.

*When is too late too late? It all depends on
what we accumulate Time cannot be collected;
only remnants of what we have wasted Unseen,
yet it is measured by light and darkness; it is reassured*

*Family time to us brings delights;
our parents tell each to avoid fight
Gathering picture of memories to
view for the few who come to visit
Never waste time today; once time is gone,
it is like a runaway*

*Time may bring us joy or sorrow,
no warning today or tomorrow To all,
be constantly amiable; by your words,
be gentle always You will never know
the person you hurt is filled with much sorrow*

*Time will eventually expire,
so do not procrastinate your desire
While there is still time,
try to mend those broken family bond
Once all the time is gone in death,
repentance is hard to undone*

Unselfish Reasons

Occasionally, I think of how I ended up in America. I never wanted to leave my family, but I did so that I could help my family. It caused my parents anguish, especially my dad. He protested my decision to leave home, but I was determined. He had no choice but to bless my decision and counseled me always to pray and inform them if things were not working out. I promised him I would, of course. Of course, I never told him the truth when things went bad after I got here. I did not want to worry him, and I knew that he would try and find a way to bring me back home. Jason Momoa's movie Sweet Girl inspired me to write this poem. His daughter in the film sacrificed to atone for what had happened to her mother.

She never contradicted before,
but she felt obligated to undo
a mistake from the past
Constantly weighing heavily on her mind,
she wished something better for her family
She resisted to avoid the pain,
like a knife being twisted on her chest that's lodge forever

Relieving every decision, she made, although
she was not asked to do, with endless regrets
Task after task, she did it without complain,
she just bowed her head to be submissive
This continued with no change and doing
what seems to be the best at that moment

Brutal winds blew her to a far away,
yet she managed to hold tight, she needed to do it
With her spirit broken into tiny pieces,
without hesitation, she would do it
do it again if needed
Relentless in her pursuit to succeed,
one day her eyes opened and saw the real picture

Gathering every strength left on her body,
she knew she had to make another resolution
But this time, she would not allow anyone to
dominate her life and would be unstoppable
She walked away and never looked back;
leaving behind her past life filled with abuse and control

Damien Bray

*J*ason and Blaine had a Meili Tour in Chicago, and I was fortunate enough to attend the event and meet them. My friends from Chicago had reserved a bottle of Meili for me to participate in the signing. I was overjoyed that Lenny and Danny had thought of me. Being there was a dream come true because I met one of Jason Momoa's friends and a brother, as he would call him. His name is Damien Bray.

Initially, I hesitated to ask him for a selfie, but my true self took over. I was so brave and asked him if he didn't mind taking a selfie with me. He happily agreed, saying, "Sure!" Oh my goodness! I was so excited. When he approached me, he politely took my camera, and I asked if I could hug him. That's when I felt his genuine warmth and kindness. It was the highlight of my visit to Chicago. I felt so grateful to have met him. As a Jason Momoa fan, I care deeply about his well-being. Three other girls share my love for him, and Irina prays for his safety every day.

Damien started his career as a stuntman in the movie industry and worked hard to become a producer after being surrounded by talented actors and producers. He's incredibly determined because he's come so far through his dedication and perseverance, overcoming any obstacles that might have hindered his success. He's truly fascinating.

Again, I'm so blessed to say that being a fan of Jason Momoa and supporting his vision and mission of cleaning the ocean has led me to meet incredible people like Damien. I would love to see them again. They should come to my area for their tour. I wanted to express my gratitude to Damien, so I even wrote him a poem.

*Your given name originated from a place
where ancient remains still stand
Architectural relics reveal its heritage and
history of the people in their land
The meaning means strong and courageous;
always lending a helping hand*

*Those who are blessed with your presence are
favored with your devotion
You are indeed an epitome of a true friend;
your loyalty is without a question
Your pleasant demeanor is substantial to
change those with bad disposition*

*Damien, you have touched many lives,
influencing them with your actions
You shower them with your undivided
attention opening their emotions
You leave everyone you meet with sense
of peace after your conversations*

*Aquaman is powerful under the sea,
but you have your strength in the land
You complete his life away from his Kingdom;
you help him in his command
With you on his side, nothing is impossible to
achieve just like a magic wand*

I need your spirit too brother; my great mission
on Earth, to Aquaman assist
We both love him Damien Bray,
so please allow me to help him,
I really insist
Two is greater than one; imagine the three of us,
many things can be done

Marvin Muth

Marvin Muth is a friend of Jason's and a music producer from Germany. His credits include music from Aquaman, Fast X, and the Minecraft movie. Like his friend Marvin, he supports The Coral Gardeners, a group that helps protect and restore coral reefs. Marvin Muth is a great man. He has a great disposition, which makes him so lovable. I even convinced him to be my pretend brother. He runs a store of vintage and antique collectibles. As a teen, he used to go with his father to Flea markets, which taught him how to recognize vintage products so well. He always has a smile on his face.

It is not a surprise that you are a great fan and
a friend of Aquaman
Your name means a "friend of the Sea"
according to God's scriptures
Perfectly chosen for you by your parents,
a perfect translation of you

You have many strengths you learned from
the man who raised you
He was a great teacher and father,
preparing you to for your destiny
Marvin means smart and quick to
learn independence at a young age

Your loyalty is unmatched,
it is rare that not many of us have such
Consistently helping your family and
friends that you always practice
You are like a brother to me that
I wished for during my childhood

Trustworthy and kind,
you gained popularity in your homeland
Your sincerity as you deliver
your speech makes you win respect
I am so grateful we became siblings,
because we share a Superhero

Slash

Slash, a global icon, holds a special place in the hearts of fans like Jason, who showcased his talent in his HBO Max streaming series, "On the Roam." With numerous musical accolades and induction into the Rock and Roll Hall of Fame in 2012, Slash's versatility as a guitarist knows no bounds. He effortlessly traverses every genre, making him a true musical maestro. It was Slash's guitar skills that ignited my passion for Guns and Roses, and Jason's admiration for him is evident in his rave reviews on the Jimmy Kimmel Show, promoting Aquaman. As a soloist, Slash's music truly captivates, and I share Jason's reverence for him. Slash's giftedness as a guitarist is undeniable, and I find solace in listening to their timeless classic, "November Rain," alongside my personal favorite, "This I Love." It's only fitting that I dedicate this poem to Jason and my musical idol, Slash.

In your premortal existence,
you were chosen to be born in these later days
A valiant spirit that God sent to earth;
you would become the musical model
Despite the tribulations you would encounter,
your dedication would prevail

Your genetic background is the
source of your rare talent and perseverance
At a young age, you met various kinds of
talented artists as your influences
These extraordinary people would
help in your journey to fulfill your dream

Music is your first love; you were predestined
to become a great musician
Your fingers were made to glide swiftly
as you create magnificent sounds
Producing marvelous music comes easy to you;
love original masterpieces

Although you received many awards in music,
you are not pompous, so humble
You show your appreciation and love that you
have for all your fans with care
Your fans adore you; young and old know,
you leave them feeling mesmerized

You defy the pre-notion on men as "playboys";
you are a faithful husband
You have many qualities and traits
distinct from people in your environment
A special woman who loves you unconditionally
would also be devoted to you

With you as precedent, your children would
develop their own love for music
Your unequivocal attributes would invoke
their choice of musical instruments
Slash, you will always shine above everyone
else for you are the chosen one

Todd Puma

I'm a huge fan of Jason Momoa, and I've always wanted to play a Gibson Les Paul like him. However, I've never owned or played a Gibson Les Paul, which is arguably the most sought-after guitar in the music industry. Les Paul was a legendary singer and guitarist, and Gibson, the company that designed the guitar, named it after him. Gibson Les Paul guitars are renowned for their distinctive clean sound, which is a favorite among electric guitar players.

One of the key features that sets Les Paul guitars apart from their competitors is their use of double coils, also known as humbuckers, for their pickups. This technology gives Les Paul guitars a unique tone that many musicians find irresistible. While Les Paul guitars are known for their high price point, they are considered a valuable investment for guitar collectors.

I recently had the opportunity to chat with fellow Jason fans on Instagram and meet one of the most prominent guitar collectors in the world. His name is Todd Puma, but he's also known as Puma in the music industry. Puma owns three Gibson Les Paul guitars that were used by the iconic band Guns N' Roses. Among his collection, the Gibson Les Paul guitars are the most valuable.

Despite his wealth and fame, Puma is a humble man. I feel incredibly fortunate to have known him. I thought it would be a great honor to write a poem in his name, as he shares his incredible guitar collection on his Instagram account. For those who may not be able to afford to own a Gibson Les Paul, we can still appreciate the beauty of these guitars by watching Puma's posts on Instagram. I thoroughly enjoy checking out his daily posts, and it's a real treat to see such a remarkable collection.

*What an honor for me to know him; his passion
and respect to an exceptional "Toys for big boys",
Gibson Les Paul guitars
These are not just ordinary toys; these are
works of art from gifted people,
creations that produce magical sounds of music
Depending on the artist's rendition,
it can evoke deep emotions within ourselves,
many types of feelings like love and anger
It represents a language awakening souls for
both young and old, creating bonds which
could last in their lifetime of existence*

*As the biggest guitar collector, Puma shows no
arrogance when sharing these beauties to his
followers of social media account
He is so humble owning pieces previously owned
by popular musicians; unselfish to display
as tribute to these famous guitarists
My heart is full of gratitude to him for I
may never own one, but he made it possible
for me to see and admire my dream guitar
He has many commendable traits,
one which delights me the most is his
sincere gratitude to his follower's reaction on his posts*

My childlike attitude comes out naturally,
even if I do my best to hold it back;
Puma is polite, he noticed comments I posted
His reaction to my childish behavior
gained him more respect by saying that
he enjoyed reading it, showing approval
We have something in common,
our love for God; he believes that
praying is important for all to
practice in our daily lives
I could go on and on describing Puma,
but there are not enough adjectives
available to portray the real Todd Puma

Sensei Matiku

When I first saw Sensei Matiku, I was impressed with his muscles. I used to do weightlifting in college, and I know what dedication it takes to reach that level. At the time, my goal was not to increase muscle mass, just for better muscle toning. I couldn't see myself looking so muscular. Being a fan of Jason Momoa, I get to meet cool people who each have their passions, such as Sensei's weightlifting. I love Sensei Matiku like a baby brother, but he is a giant beside me. It is a bit funny for me to picture myself standing beside him. He could pick me up with his fingers if I misbehaved and sit me down in timeout.

*First glance at your name, I was wondering
about your origin
You have a name with diverse meanings,
so where do I begin?
God favored me for sure to meet
you in a social media setting
It matters not to me for you are a
blessing dropped from heaven*

*You are genuinely amazing; my being
talkative did not irritate you
A childish woman who impulsively approached you,
total stranger
Instead of being perturbed, you politely
responded and said "hello"
You are so indulging and very patient with me,
a juvenile so nosey*

*Robust with a towering height,
I was hesitant to contact you at first
The feelings of dreadfulness prevented me
from messaging you
What is if you ignore me or maybe
even get annoyed with me?
But the real me came out and bravely
left you a message anyway*

My instinct was correct; you were so amiable,
I was very ecstatic
Inside a man with buffed muscles was
a sweet and gentle spirit
Devoid of arrogance, humble and
accommodating to an adult child
I knew then that you would become my Sensei,
my baby brother!

You see Sensei, you are a representation of
greatness and loyalty
When you set goals, it would always
result in enormous success
God gifted you with many talents and ideals;
you never have doubts
Your mind is as powerful as your body;
so, you will always triumph

One of your best traits is your ability to
behave like a child, humble
Children are innocent; they are forgiving;
they enjoy being playful
You make people happy just like me,
because you are full happiness
I am so grateful you agreed to be
my Sensei, brother, and my friend

Les Paul, My Eternal Love

Until I was introduced to Todd Puma, I would not have thought to write a poem about my favorite electric guitar, a Gibson Les Paul. Todd Puma's extensive collection of this fantastic guitar inspired me to write this poem. He is so awesome for sharing his collections because it allows us fans of Gibson to see the elegance, beauty, and craftsmanship of those exquisite guitars Puma has been blessed to acquire from many famous musicians. As I have mentioned earlier, he is a humble and God-loving man. I love people who always honor God, for he is, after all, our maker and the one who gifted all of us with our different talents.

I call Les Paul my Eternal Love. I love the sound of a Les Paul. The first Les Paul was made in 1952, but the best one was produced in 1959, just like me. The '59 is one of the most sought-after by musicians, along with the '57, '58, and '60. What a blessing indeed to know Todd Puma. I love going through his posts. I had the privilege of chatting with him, and we talked about Les Paul guitars. I have always commented on his posts and am so enthusiastic about how much I love them.

*I remember my first crush vividly as
a small child like it was yesterday
While others were busy at the school playground,
I was with my crush
Trying to find the best spot to sit with him,
my heart was racing to play
At age seven, I would not leave him behind
when every time I left home
I had to be with him "Twenty-four seven"
or I could not focus in my class
My crush was my confidant, my best friend,
and was always by my side*

*"Little girls should always be proper"
my mom reminded me this every day
As for me, making my crush a priority
as I started my day and off, we go
I have been improper, but always glad
to be situated on the ground
The moment I found the right spot,
I immediately played with my crush
My crush never disappointed me;
he was always there to hug and play
For a long time, I held on to my crush;
no one could ever replace him*

My dad gave me my crush;
he specially ordered for my tiny little fingers
He handed it to me on my natal day;
it was such a great birthday gift!
It was unbelievable and so incredible;
I felt so loved by his surprise present
He showed me three chords that day;
I was so eager and ready to practice
My father reminded me to do homework first,
then play it after I got done
I always made sure that all my chores were done;
it made my mother happy

Then one day, I turned into a little lady;
the day my father dreaded to come
Even my mom was not delighted for she knew
I would never act like a lady
I learned to wander further from my home;
she was mad, and I was also sad
My crush became too small for me;
I grew up tall; my crush stayed the same
Then I decided it's time for me to let my crush rest;
thinking it was the best
My heart cried as I placed my crush
in one corner of our home and alone

While walking around the neighborhood,
I saw my uncles and cousin play
I decided to join them, and I got the chance to play;
they had a huge smile
It was nice playing one I could
comfortably hold, easier to learn and play
I never forgot my old crush,
because he was my first one, my "puppy love"
So, I continued to play each day;
I made sure to do all my assigned chores
Learning new chords was so exciting;
I learned many of the popular songs

As a teenage rebel, I visited venues
that musicians hang out and played
That is where I found my true love;
was love at first sight for me
Once I found my true love,
I never wanted anyone else to be mine forever
I dreamed about him every night and day,
something so beautiful to hold
Oh, Les Paul! I am in love with you;
you are my first love and forever will be
Am I obsessed with you? Oh no I am not;

I am loyal to my eternal love
Although I may never get to hole you in my arms,
but my love is forever
I may play others and even keep them,
but you have occupied my heart
We shared your special day in 1959;
what a glorious day for musicians
I knew I was taken when we first met;
no other could ever replace you
In my lifetime, I have met so many handsome ones,
it is you am in love
Les Paul, please just wait for me;
soon I would come to finally have you

I will always have a strong desire for you;
not even time could fade it away
We have that unseen bond that exists,
and nobody could ever destroy it
I see your presence everywhere there is music;
like you are following me
That's not the case at all;
it is I who follow you and find you in our domain
So, I beg you to never give up on me;
I would hold you in my arms soon
And when that day finally comes,
we would celebrate it like humbuckers

Infatuation

Sometimes, I get unexpected declarations of admiration from men for me. It's usually the result of my overly active mouth. My uncles used to tell me that I came out of my mother's womb talking. It used to make me laugh so hard. I am very talkative, no doubt. If asked to lecture in class, I could keep it up all day without running out of topics or things to say. When talking with others, no matter the topic of conversation, I almost always have some story from my life that I can relate. The poem Infatuation is about a friend of a friend of Jason. We met accidentally, and I was unaware he knew Jason, even indirectly. He was standoffish the few times we texted each other regarding business. Then, one day, he expressed how he thought I was attractive and felt so comfortable with me. I just smiled to myself.

Infatuation can really feel so authentic;
it can strike you like a boxer
The pain can be heart wrenching;
excruciating that it leaves you fallen
Worse than being in love;
the feeling you get is deceitful in all facets
You are not really in love;
it is a false romance, true love never fades

Infatuation happens quick like a bolt of lightning;
it aims for the heart
Innocent and naive mortals are easily victimized,
but not intentionally
Long periods of solitary life are an easy target,
loneliness, an easy trap
Invoking that hidden desire of wanting to be loved,
hopeless romantic

It is like an illusion of a snake bitten person;
the venom quickly travels
The victim feels off balance from the poison's effect,
haziness occurs
Decision making gets cloudy;
the infatuated being, becomes indecisive
Obsession may even happen;
strong desire of closeness never leaves

The agonizing feeling is one sided;
it does not affect the other person
It might even make one look selfish and unfeeling:
so cruel to watch
But it is an unfair assessment of a situation
on the side of the admired
May the infatuation eventually become
mutual so both may feel joy

Molen

So-called "Hot Hunk" actors like Jason Momoa attract all sorts of fans on social media. Women can be just as easily excited as men. The comments and posts I've seen on some social media communities and fan clubs proved that point with how they made me blush! Jolene is a friend I made when we both got invited to one such raunchy fan club while we were still naive to such things. The atmosphere was not our forte, so the membership was very short-lived. Thankfully, the friendship was not. This is for her.

Don't let that vivacious and seductive pose deceive you
It could be a trick to lure you into her world filled with lies
Flowery words are spoken to gain your loyalty and respect
Be cautious, learn to discern form every step she takes

Identifying genuine stones requires patience and skills
Patience is a virtue you need to acquire the ability to win
Strategic ideas are crucial, ensuring acuity as you move
Do not allow your knight to advance without adeptness

Sly like a fox, she is indeed cunning enough to fool one
Her moves are rehearsed as often to achieve perfection
Double your efforts; master your own skills to be crafty
As you block her moves, keep her away from victory

The Canvas

Drew Barrymore, a renowned celebrity, is a vocal supporter of Jason Momoa's Mananalu Water. She proudly carries his water in her fridge at work, showcasing her dedication to the project. During a guest appearance on her show, Jason expressed his gratitude for her support, highlighting the significance of Mananalu Water.

Beyond her advocacy for Jason's project, Drew Barrymore is also known for her close friendship with Keanu Reeves. These two actors, known for their kindness and caring nature, have inspired me to write a heartfelt poem in Drew's honor.

Drew Barrymore's journey to stardom began with her iconic role in the movie E.T., where her screams captivated audiences. Growing up in the movie industry, Drew's childhood was far from ordinary. She navigated the media spotlight under the constant gaze of the public, a unique experience that shaped her into the remarkable person she is today.

Beyond her acting prowess, Drew Barrymore is a true inspiration. She has leveraged her talent to create a successful

TV show, showcasing her versatility and dedication to her craft. As one of my favorite female actresses, alongside Angelina Jolie and Sandra Bullock, Drew's contributions to the entertainment industry are undeniable.

Drew's friendship with Cameron Diaz is also noteworthy. Cameron played a pivotal role in Drew's recovery, offering her unwavering support during a challenging time. Drew's appreciation for Cameron's kindness and assistance is evident in her past statements.

Drew Barrymore's impact on my life cannot be overstated. Her warm and compassionate spirit resonates with me whenever I watch her show, leaving me in awe of her genuine nature.

*There's no adjective that I can possibly harness to
paint the portrait of real you
Your life is analogous to one of my favorite songs;
my words are so inadequate
How can I paint the portrait of a woman
who has been robbed of her childhood?*

*Your purity was ripped early;
you should have played with children of your age
A guardian failed to keep you safe;
your sweet soul was exposed to gloom
How can a protector neglect a gift from God,
a precious child, so extraordinary*

*Little mortals can't be alone with no adult guidance;
can easily be manipulated
Mingling with multitude under the influence of
toxic elements can be dangerous
How indeed did you survive treading around places not safe, unfit
for little ones*

*But I must attempt to do a portrait of your life,
even if my illustration is not perfect
One day, a knight would snatch you away from
a place to mend broken beings
So sad to be brilliant and left alone in
a place not suited for your advance mind*

He would show you a different world where
darkness ends, and light takes hold
You would experience a moment of peace,
smell of fresh air, beautiful scenery
He knows your sorrow and pain;
he would ensure that you would get proper care

God is the giver of miracles and would assist you;
I would then be able to paint you
Yes, you would have trials and tribulations;
your tenacity would bring you success
There would be few compassionate
friends to help you as you find your way back

You hate rehabilitation, refuse counsel and
would struggle to escape from the cage
Even a bird wants its freedom;
you want the same chance to fly far away to freedom
When you get out, you would find places
where people congregate without purpose

You would be spinning out of control and unstoppable;
with danger lurking nearby
Then your knight and his armor would show up and
take you to his place to safety
He would introduce you to his world full of delight and joy,
where you will feel free

Then my canvas will be ready for me to use and
paint the portrait of the hidden gem
You have waited too long filed with obstacles,
now I am ready to paint my subject
I would paint a transformation of a shattered
woman named Drew and now anew

The Sunshine of my Life

My son Justin Ian Klemann is the sunshine of my life. When I see him, it is like I have my own Jason Momoa at home. He is tall like Jason and so very talented as well. He plays percussion, guitar, keyboard, and Chess. Jason loved playing Chess with Wolf as a child. I did the same with my son. Justin loves all sorts of games now, especially tabletop games that can be played in a large group, where he can express his innate creativity and sociability. I am so proud of my son and how mature and responsible he grew up to be despite the many difficulties we had in our lives when he was younger. Jason Momoa is my twin in many ways. He was very hands-on with his children when they were younger. I did the same thing. I believe us both being Leos contribute to many of our similar traits and behaviors. When I see videos of Jason trying to play jokes with his friends, it reminds me of myself. The only difference is that I am a female but love to dress up like a boy most of the time.

My life would be so dark without you in it for you are
the sun who brings so much light
You make me smile every time you call me "mama",
like music playing my favorite classical tunes
I would be lost without you;
from the moment you came to Earth,
I knew you were a miracle

God must love me so much for allowing you
to be my son and showered you with talents
There was never a dull moment when you were a child;
you were eager to learn new things
As a two-year-old, you showed your love for drums,
when you gathered my pots and pans

You were very active and always curious about things
around you that you asked many questions
I became a great researcher and a teacher,
because you didn't just asked me simple inquiries but hard
It seemed God gifted you a brain more advanced that mine;
I had to read more to properly answer you

Playing Chess was one of your favorite games to play;
I had to quickly learned the moves to play
Reading books was also one of your interests;
you and sissy were alike so it was interesting
You always complained when sissy took too long to
finish a book, you couldn't wait your turn

As a family, the bookstore was our weekend
activity before we go dine at our favorite place
You would check all the new books that comes out
and then visit the older ones on display
At the end, we end up with few books to take home
and you get so excited, eager to go home

Oh, my sunshine! What a happy life I had when you
and sissy were at home with me in the past
You love all that I did; always asking to help
and you learned many skills you now use as an adult
The best time we had were playing our music
on the weekends at home from morning till evening

Now that you have your own home,
I miss you so much and the great
time we had with music
I wish that one day we can play again,
you in your throne making
loud noises with your drums
And I would play my guitar and sing our theme song,
Tie A Yellow Ribbon, a song we both love

My Linz

Like Jason, I also have two children, a boy and a girl. My daughter, Lindsey, is the eldest, like Lola. I was possibly overly protective of both my children. Like many new parents, I was excessively worried about my first child. I was very strict about who was allowed to care for her. I even brought her to class with me while attending nursing school. She was so intelligent and well-behaved as a toddler that the school President approved my request to let her sit in class with me. She was in school with me every day. On weekends, when I worked, she came with me as well. I was so fortunate that she was a well-behaved child. This poem is for you, my baby girl.

As if it was only yesterday when
I first held you in my arms
You were the most precious being
that my eyes saw on Earth
Fresh from God's presence,
you came to me perfect and pure
Your essence filled the room,
friends and family were waiting
I was overjoyed to finally see
the life who grew inside of me
The anxiousness, pregnancy blues,
and uneasiness were gone

I gave you a name which means
peaceful and chosen, its true
When I focused my eyes on you,
peace transpired in my heart
The loneliness that I used to feel,
disappeared, no more sadness
Every day, I looked forward to
our playtime, making memories
I read your nursery thymes,
and sang you lullabies till you sleep
Looking peaceful and calm,
I intensely watched you slumbered

I made you beautiful dresses with
matching hair bows to wear
Took you for piano lessons and
ballet classes, made you excited
So inquisitive, you asked me questions
all day, I enjoyed them all
Cat and dogs, rabbits and hamsters,
you loved having your pets
At age three, your enjoyed bedtime stories,
you always insisted
Not only one, or two, but more than three,
you never got tired

Then one day you grew so tall,
no longer her mommy's little girl
In high school, you attended prom and
hang out with your friends
You received awards, won a beauty contest,
you even did modeling
I was sad you grew up so fast,
then you started to work and dated
Eventually got a marriage proposal,
which I was reluctant to agree
My dear Linz, I miss you so much,
I pray to God we will meet again

Missing you

*A*nother short poem I wrote for my son, who is my pride and joy. I saw a picture of Jason's son, Wolf, in one of my files. Seeing his picture made me miss my son. Although this poem is short, I was so happy to write it. I love my miracle child so much, and it pains me greatly that I get to see and speak to him so rarely. The sudden memory that was spiked by that photo overwhelmed me with emotion. That day, I felt so much love and an ache from being apart from my son that I had to try to call him immediately. I cried after we talked.

I decided to call you at your workplace one day
At first, I hesitated, thinking you might really hate it
But I gathered my nerves, then bravely called you

You heard your phone ringing, and you answered
"Hello, my son, it's your mom, I miss you so much"
You responded "Oh! Hi mom, what can I do for you?"

"I just called to say I love, and I miss you son" I said
Then he told me "Thank you and I love you too mom."
He added "I have to go for now, but we will talk again."

My Baby Daiana

This poem is for Daiana. One of the many blessings I have received since I opened my Instagram account supporting Jason Momoa's Making Waves challenge is the wonderful people I have met and friends I have made. Daiana is one of the best and is like a daughter. I needed to write this poem for her because she makes me happy every time we have a video call. I know that God brought us together for a reason. Like me, Dianna is also determined to help Jason #MakeWaves. She and I know that if we don't start taking better care of our ocean and work to heal the damage already done, future generations will have to fear the ocean's wrath instead of enjoying its beauty.

You are indeed a divine being that our
Heavenly Father sent to help me
In Greek mythology, you are portrayed as a
"huntress", fast and strong
I dreamed of having many children,
especially daughters, I have you too
Your smile alone makes my day,
it erases every stress I have that day

It seems peculiar how we miss each other,
even though we just talked
We hate saying goodnight or goodbye
after having a chat with you
You manage to always send one more word,
even when told to sleep
We just can't get enough of each other;
I miss you and you miss me too

Even when we're sad, it's not so bad;
as soon as we chat, we laughed
Daily we both check to see if one was active,
immediately said hello
Your laughter is soothing to my ears,
that my anxiety would go away
We laugh even before we say anything;
it's fascinating, I find it amusing

Daiana, please don't ever leave me;
my life would dull without laughter
Since you appeared, I look forward to my nights,
my mornings are bright
You are truly my baby, because
I feel your love like you came from me
The day you said, "Goodnight mama",
we sealed the deal to be a family

Mae

*I*n the Aquaman franchise, Jason's father is played by actor Temuera Morrison. He has a cousin named Mae, whom I have met through Instagram. I have been lucky to enjoy chatting with her and even video-calling her occasionally. We are alike. We are both outgoing and positive people. She is honest, authentic, compassionate, and, most of all, has a great sense of humor. I can truly feel her love when we talk. Mae is also special to me, so I wrote a poem for her.

You always put a smile on my face every time we talk
It seems we never ran out of topics to discuss, then laugh
I love that you are so sweet, so genuine and honest to me
Even if it hurts, we tell each other the truth to protect us
We don't communicate often, but we enjoyed it, when we did

You were a great surprise to me from Heaven, marvelous
Without warning, you gave me a heartfelt compliment
I was puzzled, but you told me why before I could ask
From your side of the world of the world I gained a friend
Our friendship turned into a sisterhood, never for granted

Mae, you brought much joy in my heart; I love you sissy
No, it's not by blood, yet we love each other like we are
I know our dream will come true, what jovial day it will be
We will do the things we talked about and ride everywhere
It would be such a blast to be around you my sister Mae

Riska

*I*f you love cats, Riska is the person for you. She has fifteen cats! The cats are so spoiled that they have their own bedroom with a shower. If the way she cares for her cats didn't already make it obvious, let me assure you that she is one of the most kind and loving people I have met on Instagram. She has never missed a day without calling and checking on me. We became very close in a short time. We call each other sissy, and her daughter calls me auntie. I am so blessed to have my community of Jason fans on Instagram. Through the community, I have started to build my own small collection of followers and friends through my account, which I call my IG Family.

You are what your name means,
for you are a peace-loving person
Beauty is just an added gift that
God gave you, you are so courageous
You take risk in your life to make sure
that you would be successful
The many talents bestowed to you by our
Lord are very invaluable
You have utilized them with many
ventures in the past and present

You are a blessing to me, you became my sister,
you take it seriously
I love you for who you are to me and
for making me feel like blood
Your name also means blood and
for me a symbol of true sacrifice
In your life, you endured so many tribulations,
yet you never gave up
The love you have for your
daughter inspires you to remain strong

We call each other sissy like
we have known each other all this time
You constantly remind me of the
positive side of life, you love deeply
When I am depressed, you cheer me up,
you make me laugh and smile
We share our bad and good days;
we love to inspire, lift each other up
Thank you, my sissy, for your love
and kindness, I love you eternally

My French Angel

A French lady complimented my Recycled Fashion post, making me elated. She seemed genuine and asked if she could call me Lily. I agreed. When researching Lily's meaning in French, I discovered that lilies symbolize purity. I knew the beautiful French lady sensed my spirit, not just what could be seen on the screen, and we shared that same gift. Her name is Nad and this poem is for her.

Meeting you was more than a great surprise, a blessing
I never imagined a stranger would give sincere admiration
Fashion designing and music are two of my favorite hobbies
To be admired by a French woman means so much to me

When it comes to fashion, no one excels better, but them
From perfumes to fashions, they are always on the top
Your compliments to my work gave me self confidence
The ordinary me? This can't be real, I am not that great

My angel, you constantly did it, I started to wonder if it's real
So, I ask your name and for a picture; you are so beautiful
I couldn't believe the gorgeous woman gave me compliments
I couldn't thank you enough, because I felt the sincerity in you

You inspired me even more. I eagerly searched for more
Every material I see, I would imagine how it would look
My mind was busy creating fashions to mix and match
My French Angel, you are my friend, my sister in this world

One day when we finally see each other, we will celebrate
For God brought us together, so I can create more fashion
To give me more confidence which I lacked from the start
Now, I do it with ease and no obstacles too hard to cross

Lenny and Danny

I was ecstatic when my husband surprised me with a trip to see Jason Momoa in Miami for their Meili Vodka tour. There were two event dates that weekend, and we missed the first because we didn't get there early enough, so the line was already hundreds of people long. For the second event, we played it safe and arrived so early that I was among the first 20 in line. In that early morning line, there were two young men just ahead of me in line. As we talked away the long wait, I learned how friendly and kind the boys are. Without them, my husband would have been exhausted checking on me every half an hour to ensure I was all right and did not need anything. He is generally shy, tired from all the driving, and has no desire to meet Jason. These two young men offered my husband that they would look out for me and make sure I ate and took my medicine.

We had such a great time waiting in line. A few days after the event, when they arrived home in Chicago, I received a video call from them. Their friends and Danny's girlfriend, Dania, were included in the call. It is so amazing the bond we developed for each other. When Jason Momoa was scheduled to go to Chicago for a Meili Tour, they immediately sent me the event date poster and invited me to come with them.

Two young men, I encountered in line, they were so fine
Lenny was the serious kind and Danny was the playful
When Danny misbehaved, Lenny would yell at Danny
But Danny can't help it; his contradiction is innocent

Danny is always preoccupied with his enthusiastic mind
He loves to see women's eyes; to him they are fascinating
Lenny love to converse, so we discussed numerous topics
I enjoyed them both for they kept me smiling, never boring

Lenny loves meeting celebrities and travels just to see them
The two are like brothers, so Danny comes along with Lenny
In them, I saw genuine love; becoming their friend was a bliss
I never met young men like Lenny and Danny, so kind to me

Both invited me to see Jason Momoa's Meili Tour in Chicago
Andy trusts them both to take care of me away from my home
I know God also sent me trustworthy young men, so to rare find
My love for Lenny and Danny will never be fade, even with time

Luke and Vincent

*T*hese two incredibly talented young men, Luke and Vincent, became my Instagram family because of my passion for playing the guitar. Luke discovered me first and then encouraged his friend Vincent to follow me. When we first met, I was strumming my guitar and singing an old song. Through messaging about music, we quickly formed a deep friendship. Luke has an old soul, and most of the songs he plays are ones I've loved for even longer than he's been alive. They've become like my nephews in the Philippines. Like them, they also play the guitar, and when I visit them, we gather and play our favorite songs together.

Young and talented, that's what make them close to my heart
While most of their peers love new pops, theirs are the past
I love them love them just like my nephews who also play guitar
Luke saw me sang, played the song I used to play for my dad
What a joy to meet him, a reminder of my son, also a musician
Later, Vincent followed me just like Luke, they are best friends

We don't chat or talk as often as my other family, it's alright
I always remind them to focus on school first, then music next
As a mother of two, I counseled them the same things I gave mine
I even joined my children playing music, after all chores are done
Meeting them both gave me much delight, like having kids again
I make time to check them on them both, to make sure they are fine

My heart softens, when I meet children with sweet soul
Luke and Vincent might be young, but they are very mature
Respectful and polite, they never fail to express their thanks
I almost wish they were my own children, silly for me to think
They are members of my Instagram family, fills me with delight
I feel so blessed to know them, excellent examples of great youths

My IG Family

S ocial media can be challenging sometimes. It is a place where cyber criminals love to surf and find innocent people to scam. It can be a great way to advertise businesses and promote all types of commercial services and not for profit organizations. When I decided to open an account for the Mananalu Water founded by Jason Momoa, I wanted my social account to have a different culture. I was not concerned about having the number of followers, but the quality. It is why I created it to offer a more friendly environment. To implement my concept, it had to start with me, the creator of my verified page. I was very observant of the individuals and groups who were following me. It is hard to discriminate between your followers based on their positive or negative traits. It takes several interactions to know someone in a social media environment. Eventually I met great people. Some are so thoughtful and caring. I was interested in those types of followers. Eventually I formed my own Instagram family within my account. I was thinking that instead of giving out some kind of badge to my loyal followers, turning them into my family was a better choice. It gives everyone a sense of belonging. These are individuals who became so close to me that we are in constant communication. There are three of them who enjoy video calling. All my small, but quality family never failed to immediately send me messages asking if I was alright. We check on each other and I, as the account holder, try my best to give them my undivided attention. We try to be supportive to our IG Family members. We are all Jason Momoa's fans; therefore, our goal is to help promote his pet project, cleaning the ocean.

I would like to mention my members and write a brief description regarding how they came to be my family. My first one was Irina, through the tribute reel I created for Travis Snyder's passing. She saw the reel I created as a tribute to him. Jason was away promoting his movie Aquaman 2 and I felt it was my job to do it, since he was away. I know how hurt he must have been losing his best friend who is like his sibling. I was so devastated when I saw the post announcing his death, I cried. Irina cares so much for Jason and his vision and mission like I do. So, we had that in common. It did not take long for us to be close and call each other almost daily. We have many things in common. She has two children, both girls. She works as a Registered Nurse, which was my first major in college until I changed to business administration. Music, a huge one in common, but she is so talented in piano too and singing. We are both hyper and very talkative. We love joking around and also we get serious when needed.

The next one I would love to mention is Riska, who calls me daily. We are like real sisters, and I love her beautiful daughter Emma. Emma is smart and talented. She calls me auntie, which makes me smile every time I hear it. Riska never misses a day without checking on me. She is aware of how painful my fibromyalgia can be. She gets concerned if I don't take time to rest. I miss her calls during Ramadan. She was unable to call me due to time difference after the long day of fasting. I can honestly say that she has filled the void of my sisters' inability to love me. They have basically abandoned me for years now. Riska too their place.

Next of my IG Family who I love so much also is Mae. She is truly a blessing to me as far as lifting my spirit. When I have emotional problems, she tries hard to make me laugh. She is not afraid to also remind me to ignore negative people. She is a very compassionate person too. When her friends require assistance, she would not ignore them. She comes to their homes and takes great care of them ensuring they have all the necessary things they need and even cleans their homes also. I cannot wait to spend time with her. She is from New Zealand. She tells me the truth, even if it hurts. That is very important in any relationship. I love her culture. I understand why Jason loves New Zealand. Honoring their culture is very important to them, as it should. I believe that culture must not be forgotten, even if we move to another country. We can still do both cultures. I have taught my children important cultures so every time we visit my birth country, they are able to practice it and my relatives appreciate them for doing so.

Ruth has fibromyalgia like me. She seldom has the time to chat or call, but always reacts to my post. She is also kind and compassionate. She loves animals and has a dog she adores. We are parents of fur babies. She loves sharing videos on animals and funny ones about certain behaviors.

Mika is from Japan. We never chat or call, but she always reacts to my post and sends me heart emojis and she plays the ukelele very well. I also feel her sweet spirit.

Edith is a graphic designer from Germany. Although we don't chat or call each other, we have an unspoken understanding of our bond as a family on Instagram. She never fails to react to my post like the rest. I can tell Edith is a great person. I love her very much.

Jane is another one I love very much. She is always happy to see my post, especially when I am singing. We seldom chat due to her schedule, but I know she thinks of me, and I do the same. She loves Jason Momoa very much as a human being and actor. Jane is so adorable and loving. She is one of my inspirations to stay active.

Myriam is another member who creates Wolves background for Jason Momoa's pictures on her account. She has a pleasant personality and reacts to my post all the time. Myriam has two girls who are still in school.

Britta is from Iceland, and I adore her. We spoke a few times, but she still works, and her schedule is hectic. She loves spending time with her family on her days off. She is very thoughtful. When she sees animals on the road, she would take a video or picture to send me. She knows I love animals. She is very thoughtful and honest too. She became very close to me quickly. I would love to visit her family someday.

Cinderella is young and she calls me auntie. She is so beautiful and has been a winner of a local beauty pageant in the past. I love her very much. We seldom talk, because she works and has a little girl. She loves talking to me, when she gets a free time. I enjoy our conversations. She calls me auntie. She always wanted to have an aunt. I feel so blessed she decided to make me one.

Ivana is another one who is also young and beautiful. She calls me mom and told me that she loves having two mothers, her biological mother and adopted mother, me. She calls or messages me from time to time. I want to visit her someday as well. I even invited her to visit me if she can get a visa. She has a child also who is in school. I can honestly say that she takes my role as her IGFamily mom seriously. She makes me so happy, because my biological daughter hasn't spoken to me for almost 20 yrs. I don't know if she ever will.

Candy is the one who I have only spoken to three times, but just like the others, I feel her sincerity and concern towards my health. She never misses reacting to my post as well. Candy was in an accident that left her paralyzed, but she is such a strong person. She never allows her situation to affect her demeanor. She gives me compliments from time to time, which makes me feel loved by her.

Daiana is from Switzerland, and she is like a daughter to me. I love having a video call with her. We both miss each other when we are not able to communicate. She loves to do photography and is talented in drawing. She works in a hospital part time doing photography for newborn babies. She makes me laugh every time we talk.

We have young men in our group, Vincent and Luke. They are also into music and that is what connected me to them. One day Luke saw my video playing my guitar and sang an old song. He followed me and then he told Vincent about it. Vincent decided to follow me as well. I love them like they are my own children. Luke is much closer to me than Vincent.

PJ is the creator of a podcast regarding Bullying and her Instagram Account is Momoa Mania. She is very close to me, because she shares her grandson with me. I learned to love her and her grandson like my blood relatives. She raised her grandson since infancy. The mother left the baby with her due to his disability. He loved being called Monkey and that is what we call him. Monkey is a very happy child, despite not being able to talk fluently. PJ is a hero to this child, and she is also my hero too. I love her and if she has free time, we try to call each other. Her show has helped some famous people overcome the effects of bullying. She does not monetize her time on this podcast. I admire her so much for that, because she could really use some extra income. I pray that she will be discovered by Jason Momoa one day. Maybe Jason can share his own experience when it comes to being bullied.

There are a few others from other countries who we welcome to our fold. Some are not fluent in English, which deter their desire to communicate with me. Yet, I feel the bond and I also tell them that I love them. If they need to discuss something with me, I give them my undivided attention. I feel so blessed to have them in my life. As Jason Momoa's fan, I feel that I should be kind to his fans. After all, I am a promoting a man who is also kind and loving. Irina and I are always praying for Jason and his family. We know that he is so busy, and he needs to be strong and healthy to accommodate many people. My Instagram family are just a few grains of sand in comparison to the rest of Jason's fans all over the world, but they are the best of the best. I am blessed to have them in my life.

King Papa

Our aunt and uncle, Kenny and Ann, recently retired in Florida. They're the most loving and caring couple I've ever met. They're incredibly supportive of my passion for Jason Momoa's Mananalu Water. Auntie Ann even calls me "Miss Mananalu."

When Jason and Blaine went to Miami for their Meili tour, they asked my husband and brother-in-law to help clean their pool. It wasn't a big deal—it took them a few minutes, but they overpaid them. That's just how generous they are.

We're always invited to dinner with them weekly, and they always prepare so much food that we take them with us. My uncle served in the Army and had such great principles in life—always being kind and honest.

As an expression of gratitude for their support, I wrote them both a poem. I explained how important it is to me that Mananalu Water eventually reaches the Philippines so Jason can also clean our ocean there. I lived near the ocean as a child and have so many fond memories of playing at the beach during low tide. We'd dig for clams and other edible sea creatures living near the shore and swim during high tide. It was such a carefree time.

I wish my nieces and nephews could have experienced the same joy and wonder I did as a child.

You insisted me calling you King papa
I gave you look, and you just stare at me
I never know if you are serious or joking
But we still come around to be with you

Your grandchildren are your whole world
No other could give you both pure joy
All it takes is a call or text from one
Silence takes over as you answer them

Your little princess, she is indeed one
Her call is the highlight of your day
Just like your wife, you are also kind
You feel sad for people to go without

King Papa is not so easy to read you
You act tough so we would feel scared
We know better, you even feed squirrels
Your fur baby is fed with the best meat

Joking around makes your delighted
You never crack a smile when you do it
Swearing up and down that it is the truth
Till your little Ken tells us the real story

Honesty is your policy and no other way
It is your belief that everyone should follow
You are fair to everyone you encounter
Sometimes you even do it much further

Kind Papa, we love and adore you much
We miss your attitude, so we come to visit
You feed us until our bellies would explode
You and your Queen love spoiling us all

Auntie Ann

Your name represents an infinite amazing adjective
There is no other like you; God broke you mold after
He molded you an epitome of love and compassion
You are also devoted, kind to everyone around you
We love you not because you're giving, you're so real
Your presence in our lives has brought us blessings

So many positive assets to mention; I will talk on few
Loving, a trait so hard many to practice, except you
You give love to everyone one like it's just pennies
Kindness, a trait so difficult to find, you do it easily
You are so magnanimous; you only see good in all
It shows in all that you do at home with your family

Compassion, a trait everyone needs to always do
You do it so well; you are quick to come to the rescue
Caring is a concern for others ensuring no one is left
You almost give too much; like the ones I received
Auntie Ann, you are like a saint, Mother Theresa
I will never encounter one I can call my auntie Ann

You would go without for your grandchildren to visit
Every mother dream to have a daughter like you
Blessed are the ones who experienced your love
You beget affection and happiness to the elderly
Some of your great traits are visible at first glance
How can we thank you for all that you do for us?

You Are Mine

As I began to gain followers who are fans of Jason, I encountered some who genuinely cared about me. Ivana had always been very kind to me from the first time we spoke. The longer I knew her, she became my daughter on Instagram. She mentioned to her biological mother that she found a mom in the USA. I told her to thank her mother for allowing me to share her daughter like my own. Ivana makes me so happy every time she leaves me messages or when we do video calls. She never forgets to tell me how much she loves me and I do the same. She told me that she would not allow any hurt any of her family, including me. So, she deserves a poem. She also told me that one day, she would visit me. I'm so elated and cannot wait to see her and my granddaughter.

How blessed I am to have you in my life;
you inspire and lift my spirit

God has blessed me with an angel,.
a daughter with the purest soul

You outer beauty is the reflection of your
the light inside your heart

My dearest baby girl, how did I get so
blessed with your our true love

When I see your smile, my heart rejoices,
I can't help myself from crying

Not tears of sadness, but overflowing
tears of the happiness from you

You love me so much like I had carried
you inside for nine months

I am complete because of you; the purest
being God sent into my life

You infused me with joy;
wiping my all my tears with your devotion

How can I ever thank you my baby girl;
to find you a gift is impossible

A match for the love you have given me is
difficult to find anywhere

All I can give you is my heart and soul,
it's yours always for eternity

Altruism

This poem hits hard to core of my soul. It was written one night as I was pondering about my role on this planet. I never second guessed myself when I decided to leave my birth place. My children became my whole life during the most trying time of my existence on Earth. This poem is also for all the mothers in the world. Our mother is our first at everything we do in life. When my daughter was born, it them that I realized the pain she had to endure having me in her womb and to deliver a child is beyond my comprehension until I became a mother myself. To all the mothers out there, this is dedicated to you.

She was chosen for a special calling on Earth
To be elected is a great honor for a spirit
Her acceptance signifies a profound love

They must have seen her many hidden talents,
For her assignment requires a Warrior's strength
Her chores will be endless and backbreaking

Then the long awaited moment finally came
As they crossed the veil, memories dissipated
She will now embark on her earthly journey

Her enormous heart gets heavy sometimes
In her mind she whispers "You cannot give up!"
Her dedication and love will give her power

She didn't know how challenging it would be
For she wouldn't remember their conversations
Now she must learn the secret to success

Her overwhelming love for them intercedes
She works hard all day and never complains
Because she is a mother, an altruistic being

Conclusion

*M*y journey with my favorite celebrity has been inspiring and exhilarating. If I had to do it all over again, I would be even more adventurous in my pursuit to help him meet his vision and mission. Cleaning our ocean is crucial to all of us, the planet Earth is now suffering from global warming and our oceans assist in the temperature equilibrium of our planet. Jason Momoa founded Mananalu Water using aluminum containers instead of plastic to bottle his products. When I heard the great news that he is using aluminum containers, I was so excited that I decided to open an Instagram account, and my husband suggested having it verified to attract great followers. We immediately ordered online for our first Mananalu Water to try at home. It tasted so great, even if you drink it unrefrigerated. I then read all I could to learn as much as I could about his product. If I had to help him with his goal in removing plastic permanently from our ocean, I needed to be educated regarding this product that I am about to promote on social media. It is crucial that I would be able to answer questions from my followers and the people that I would meet in public as I carry the water with me. There was no stopping my support for Jason Momoa making waves about this awesome water in an aluminum can. The first thing I did was take a picture of me holding the water to use as my profile picture on both my Facebook and Instagram account. Even my background on both accounts was of Jason Momoa. I wanted everyone to know I am dedicated in my pursuit to help Jason Momoa. My husband was also doing his part to assist me as far as my accounts. He is a genius when it comes to technology. He is such a great blessing in my life. I would not be able to do it without him. It was a family effort, even his brother and his best friend were very happy for me.

Why is it so important for me to spread the news to those who are not aware of the alternative? I have children and extended families here and in the Philippines. I was concerned about the future generation who would not have what we have enjoyed before them. The issue of global warming is not going away. There are so many factors affecting our current temperature equilibrium on our planet. One of the factors is the use of plastic in various businesses around the world. The increase in world population and businesses affected our ocean due to the amount of garbage that is thrown in our oceans and other types of garbage. What exactly does this garbage have to do with our Earth's temperature? Without going into a long narrative on the other factors that affect the temperature on our planet, I will focus on the use of plastic and its effects on our oceans. Plastic is not biodegradable. What does it mean exactly? Biodegradable means something that can decompose by bacteria or other types of organisms in our environment. Plastic on the other hand cannot be decomposed, even if we try to use machines to break it down. We will end up with tiny plastic or micro size plastic. Our oceans help absorb the heat from the sun that we need to also survive as inhabitants of the earth. Our planet is composed of 70% of water from our oceans. Micro plastics in the bottom of our oceans decrease the amount of heat absorption from the sun, because it blocks the bottom of the oceans and the heat remains on the top; therefore, our land would end up with the extra heat. It becomes a bad cycle. Marine animals are there to assist in making our ocean healthy and clean. Each of the marine animals has their role on our planet. One very important role of some marine animals is feeding humans and jobs. If these marine communities were destroyed due to plastics and other types of garbage, humanity would cease to exist. The extreme high temperature would destroy every living thing on earth. I would like to make one example of one important marine animal that is very crucial to all the other marine life. For example, large whales play a great role in providing nitrogen and other nutrients. Whales excretes these on the surface of the ocean. This process is called "the whale pump" providing the necessary nutrients to help in maintaining the marine life ecosystem. Whale pump is the process of excreting feces from the whale at the surface of the ocean. Their feces provide nutrients to the phytoplankton and other small marine animals like small fish and crustaceans. Krill, which belongs to the crustacean family, are a source of food for baleen whales. These whales consume tons of krill per feeding. Krill also helps in our temperature by absorbing some of the carbon emission from our atmosphere.

I am grateful for this opportunity to publish a book of poems inspired by Jason Momoa. Not only is he the founder of Mananalu Water, but he is also a great influencer in many environmental nonprofit organizations. He has so much love and respect for our planet. It is my hope that this book will be able to help Jason in his vision and mission of removing plastic from our ocean permanently. The issue of global warming is not going away. We need to all work together in trying to slow it down. Our ocean has been abused for a long period of time now. We cannot afford to delay or ignore this problem. As a fan of Jason Momoa, I am determined to do my part in spreading the use of aluminum for bottled water. Mananalu Water bottles are so practical, it is reusable, so if you want to put in your own water, you can do it. Resealable means after you open the bottle, you can use the cap to close the bottle if you want to use it again. Recyclable, after many uses, you can finally send it for recycling. Another important reason I also love Mananalu Water is their flavored ones do not have any added sugar or sweetener. Other products available in the market use artificial chemicals to make it sweet. I cannot drink any beverage with such additives. I would like to end this by expressing my sincere gratitude to Jason Momoa and his water. I will not stop my effort in spreading his concept. It is for the good of all the inhabitants on Earth and our future generation to enjoy the world beneath our land.

Biography

$\mathcal{A}$lthough born in the Philippines Ligaya (Aying) Espina Cerny has spent almost 2/3rds of her life in the United States moving to her new country at the age of 19. Appreciating how similar the climate in Florida was to the Philippines it has been her residence ever since she came to her new country In 1979. As a mother of two living in central Florida, she enjoyed taking her kids to amusement parks and the beach. Currently retired, Ligaya has worked various jobs in the medical and customer service industries. She has her bachelor's degrees in business healthcare administration as well as a degree in Radio Communication.

With a lifelong passion for music and writing both are vital parts of Aying's life. She has been an avid journal writer feeling the need to keep life's simple or great events from being forgotten. Growing up in a very musically talented family she wrote her first song with a cousin at the age of twelve. With such a creative mind whenever inspiration hits, she must write down her thoughts on whatever may be on hand be it napkins or the small notebook normally in her purse so that an idea for a new song or poem won't be lost. The dual love of writing and music has led her naturally to writing poetry where the two worlds so easily touch. She started off working on short poems and working to craft her own style. Noticing that many people are unable to appreciate poetry that is needlessly complex, Ligaya has promised herself that her poetry would be written in a simple style that could be accessible to most people.

www.ingramcontent.com/pod-product-compliance
Lightning Source LLC
Chambersburg PA
CBHW041626140626
46547CB00030B/1086